Past Praise for the KNOWING JESUS SERIES

"In true Tara-Leigh fashion, this study is easy to follow while also challenging you to dig deeper into what the Word is saying. It's more than simply reading the Bible and answering some questions. It's a test to gauge your spiritual walk, to ask the hard questions, and to be challenged with each turn of the page about what the Holy Spirit is revealing. Whether you are a new believer or well-versed in theological teachings, this study has something to offer everyone."

Clare Thompson Sims, D-Group member

"This study delivers what D-Group has been doing for years. Instead of feeding the readers answers, it empowers them to do the work of arriving at answers through the careful study and close reading of God's Word, allowing them to take ownership of their continued growth and faith in King Jesus. What a thrilling start of a memorable new series!"

Zuzana Johansen, D-Group member

"This study helps the reader connect the Old Testament with the New by giving the perspective of the Jewish culture and customs during Jesus's day. This lens provides clarity as to why Jesus ministered and spoke as He did while interacting with both Jews and Gentiles. It also clearly communicates the relevance and life-changing power of Jesus's teachings for Christians today. It's a road map, pulling from the pages of the Old Testament and connecting it to the Gospels, pointing to our victory in Christ on the cross."

Jeremy Hall, D-Group member

"*Knowing Jesus as King* combines a deep dive into the book of Matthew with the structure of D-Group. Having been in D-Group from the very start—fifteen years ago—I can confidently say the structure creates the consistency it demands and bears much fruit for any believer. Buckle up and have faith that God will reveal Himself to you as the promised and present King over the next ten weeks."

Meghann Glenn, D-Group charter member

KNOWING
JESUS
AS SERVANT

Also by Tara-Leigh Cobble

The Bible Recap:
A One-Year Guide to Reading and Understanding the Entire Bible

The Bible Recap Study Guide:
Daily Questions to Deepen Your Understanding of the Entire Bible

The Bible Recap Journal:
Your Daily Companion to the Entire Bible

The Bible Recap Discussion Guide:
Weekly Questions for Group Conversation on the Entire Bible

The Bible Recap Kids' Devotional:
365 Reflections and Activities for Children and Families

The God Shot:
100 Snapshots of God's Character in Scripture

Israel:
Beauty, Light, and Luxury

THE BIBLE RECAP KNOWING JESUS SERIES*

Knowing Jesus as King:
A 10-Session Study on the Gospel of Matthew

Knowing Jesus as Servant:
A 10-Session Study on the Gospel of Mark

*General editor

KNOWING JESUS AS SERVANT

A 10-SESSION STUDY ON THE GOSPEL OF MARK

TARA-LEIGH COBBLE,
GENERAL EDITOR

WRITTEN BY THE D-GROUP THEOLOGY & CURRICULUM TEAM

BETHANYHOUSE

a division of Baker Publishing Group
Minneapolis, Minnesota

© 2024 by Tara-Leigh Cobble

Published by Bethany House Publishers
Minneapolis, Minnesota
BethanyHouse.com

Bethany House Publishers is a division of
Baker Publishing Group, Grand Rapids, Michigan

Printed in the United States of America

Library of Congress Cataloging-in-Publication Data
Names: Cobble, Tara-Leigh, editor.
Title: Knowing Jesus as servant : a 10-session study on the Gospel of Mark / Tara-Leigh Cobble, general editor.
Description: Minneapolis, Minnesota : Bethany House Publishers, a division of Baker Publishing Group, [2024] |
    Series: The bible recap knowing jesus series | Includes bibliographical references.
Identifiers: LCCN 2023058287 | ISBN 9780764243578 (paperback) | ISBN 9781493446889 (ebook)
Subjects: LCSH: Christian leadership—Biblical teaching. | Servant leadership—Biblical teaching. | Jesus Christ—
    Leadership. | Bible Mark—Criticism, interpretation, etc.
Classification: LCC BS2555.6.L42 K66 2024 | DDC 262/.1—dc23/eng/20240223
LC record available at https://lccn.loc.gov/2023058287

Interior design by Nadine Rewa
Cover design by Dan Pitts
Author image from © Meshali Mitchell

The general editor is represented by Alive Literary Agency, www.AliveLiterary.com.

The D-Group Theology & Curriculum Team is Laura Buchelt, Emily Pickell, Meg Mitchell, Evaline Asmah, Brittney Rice, and Tara-Leigh Cobble.

Baker Publishing Group publications use paper produced from sustainable forestry practices and postconsumer waste whenever possible.

24 25 26 27 28 29 30   7 6 5 4 3 2 1

CONTENTS

INTRODUCTION

The Gospels (Matthew, Mark, Luke, and John) offer us fourfold telling of Jesus's story. Some may wonder why this is necessary, but the fascinating truth is that each gospel speaks to a specific audience and emphasizes a unique aspect of who Jesus is. Additionally, the areas where they overlap verify the authenticity of the full narrative.

Matthew writes about King Jesus—His authority, His royalty, and His throne that will last forever. Mark writes about Jesus as the Suffering Servant, the One whose suffering would eternally serve all who call on His name. Luke, drawing on Jesus's humanity, emphasizes Jesus as Savior of mankind, which seems fitting since Luke was a doctor. And John, the self-proclaimed favorite of our Lord, repeatedly highlights that Jesus is God. These four narratives help us see Jesus from various angles, capturing different facets of His glory—King, Servant, Savior/Man, God. These characteristics may seem opposed to each other, but they actually present us with a fuller understanding of who He is. All four accounts are not only necessary but beautiful!

The book of Mark is most commonly attributed to Mark, also known as John Mark, who traveled with Peter as his interpreter. Since this gospel is full of information someone would know only if they were present, scholars tend to agree that Mark was recording Peter's personal experiences with the Suffering Servant. The apostle Paul told the church in Colossae that Mark was Barnabas's cousin (Colossians 4:10), Mark makes several appearances in Acts (12:12, 25; 13:13; 15:37–40), and though he seemed to have disagreements with Paul, Mark was eventually praised by Paul in his letter to Timothy (2 Timothy 4:11).

This gospel was likely written in Rome, specifically to Gentile Roman followers of Jesus. The reason scholars think this is threefold. First, Mark translated Aramaic words for his readers (3:17; 5:41; 7:11, 34; 10:46; 14:36; 15:22, 34). Second, he used Latin expressions instead of Greek words in some places (5:9; 6:27; 12:15, 42; 15:16, 39) and referenced time according to the Roman system of the day (6:48; 13:35). Third, Mark explained Jewish customs in detail (7:3, 4; 14:12; 15:42), omitted genealogies tracing Jesus's lineage, and included fewer references to the Old Testament. These things seem to indicate he was catering to a Gentile audience.

Mark's tone is distinct as well. His stories have an urgency to them—he used the word *immediately* over forty times! Mark wrote the shortest of all the gospels—only 678 verses—but that didn't stop him from painting vivid pictures of the life of Christ. Mark's lens was Jesus as Servant, and that point is hammered home most clearly in Mark 10:45. This gospel was recorded prior to the fall of the temple in AD 70 and was likely written in the mid-to-late AD 50s, while eyewitnesses to Christ's life were still alive. It appears to have been the first gospel recorded, since we find significant overlap in the other gospels, particularly Matthew and Luke.

As you read through what may be a familiar story, challenge yourself to push past the surface to understand Mark's perspective of the life of the most important Man to walk the earth. Jesus, who is God, reigns as King and Savior, yet He came to earth as a suffering servant. Have you stopped to let that transform you? Let's begin that journey together!

HOW TO USE THIS STUDY

While Bible study is vital to the Christian walk, a well-rounded spiritual life comes from engaging with other spiritual disciplines as well. This study is designed not only to equip you with greater knowledge and theological depth, but to help you engage in other formative practices that will create a fuller, more fulfilling relationship with Jesus. We want to see you thrive in every area of your life with God!

Content and Questions

In each of the ten weeks of this study, the teaching and questions are divided into six days, but feel free to do it all at once if that's more manageable for your schedule. If you choose to complete each week's study in one sitting (especially if that time occurs later in the study-week), keep in mind that there are aspects you will want to be mindful of each day: the daily Bible reading, Scripture memorization, and the weekly challenge. Those are best attended to throughout the week.

Daily Bible Reading

The daily Bible reading corresponds to our study. It will take an average of three minutes per day to simply read (not study) the text. If you're an auditory learner, you may prefer to listen to an audio version of these Bible chapters.

Even if you decide to do the week's content and questions in one sitting, we still encourage you to make the daily Bible reading a part of your regular daily rhythm. Establishing a habit of reading the Word every day will help fortify your faith and create greater connections with God.

If you decide to break the study up into the six allotted days each week, your daily Bible reading will align with your study. Days 1–5 will follow our study of Mark, Day 6 features a psalm that corresponds to our reading, and Day 7 serves as a catch-up day in case you fall behind.

Scripture Memorization

Memorizing Scripture isn't busywork! It's an important part of hiding God's Word in our hearts (Psalm 119:11). Our passage—Mark 10:42–52—includes Jesus's mission statement on service. We encourage you to practice it cumulatively—that is, *add* to what you're practicing each week instead of *replacing* it. We quote the English Standard Version (and some of our resources are in that translation as well), but feel free to memorize it in whatever translation you prefer. We suggest working on each week's verse(s) throughout the week, not just at the last minute. We've provided some free tools to help you with this, including a weekly verse song: MyDGroup.org/Resources/Mark.

Weekly Challenge

This is our practical response to what we've learned each week. We want to be "doers of the word, and not hearers only" (James 1:22). You'll find a variety of challenges, and we encourage you to lean into them all—especially the ones you find *most* challenging! This will help strengthen your spiritual muscles and encourage you in your faith. As with the memory verse, you'll want to begin this practice earlier in the week, especially because some weekly challenges include things to do each day of the week (e.g., prayers, journaling, etc.).

Resources

This is a Scripture-heavy study, and you'll find yourself looking up passages often. If you're new to studying Scripture, this will be a great way to dig in and sharpen your skills! You will feel more equipped and less intimidated as you move through each chapter. Some questions may ask you to refer to a Bible dictionary, commentary, or Greek or Hebrew lexicon, but you don't need to purchase those tools. There are lots of free options available online. We've linked to some of our favorite tools—plus additional resources such as podcasts, articles, and apps—at MyDGroup.org/Resources/Mark.

Mark 1:
The Servant Established

Note: If you haven't yet read "How to Use This Study" on pages 11–12, please do that before continuing. It will provide you with a proper framework and helpful tools.

DAILY BIBLE READING

Day 1: Mark 1:1–8

Day 2: Mark 1:9–15

Day 3: Mark 1:16–20

Day 4: Mark 1:21–34

Day 5: Mark 1:35–45

Day 6: Psalm 85

Day 7: Catch-Up Day

Corresponds to Day 277 of *The Bible Recap*.

WEEKLY CHALLENGE

See page 33 for more information.

Mark 1:1–8

 **READ MARK 1:1-8**

1. **Review Mark 1:1.** How does the book begin?

Unlike the other three gospels, the book of Mark doesn't start with a genealogy, a theological thesis, or the birth of Jesus. *Gospel* means "the good news of the fulfillment of God's promises." And Mark begins with the gospel Himself: Jesus Christ, the Son of God.

2. **Review Mark 1:1–8. Then read Isaiah 40:3–5.** How do these passages connect?

In Roman tradition, a forerunner—also known as a herald—announced the arrival of important Roman officials. Roman Christians hearing Mark's letter would've been deeply familiar with this role. John the Baptist (we'll call him JTB) was the forerunner of Jesus, the messenger preparing the people for His arrival.

In addition to announcing the arrival of Jesus, JTB baptized people. People from Judea and Jerusalem came to the Jordan River to receive his baptism, but he called them to more than baptism itself. He called them to *repentance*.

3. **Look up *repentance* in a Bible dictionary.** Write down the definition.

4. How is repentance different from confession?

5. How is repentance different from regret?

While he baptized people and called them to repentance, he also preached, pointing them to Jesus.

6. In 1:7, what three things did JTB say about Jesus?

At the time this book was written, untying someone's sandals would have been a low-level servant's job. But knowing who Jesus was, JTB said he wasn't worthy to serve Him, even in a task as lowly as that.

7. **Skip ahead and read Mark 10:45.** How does Jesus describe Himself?

Jesus, the Son of God—whose arrival had been long awaited and prophesied, whose ministry was announced by a forerunner, whose authority is God's, and whose sacrifice makes our reconciliation with God possible—came to serve.

A lack of repentance and an inflated view of ourselves may lead us to believe that we are worthy to do much more for Jesus than untie His sandals, or even that we deserve Jesus's service to us. But when we repent and really believe that His service to us is a gift we don't deserve and could never earn, we can humbly and gratefully accept the gift of eternal life made possible through Jesus the Servant.

Although we aren't worthy to serve Him, and He doesn't need our service, He delights when we serve Him with gladness (see Psalm 100:2) and demonstrate our affection for Him!

8. What are some ways you delight to demonstrate your affection for God through service?

DAY 2

Mark 1:9–15

 **READ MARK 1:9–15**

Yesterday, we learned that JTB called the people he was baptizing to more than baptism itself: He called them to repentance.

1. **Review 1:9–11.** Why do you think Jesus—who never sinned and did not need to repent—was baptized?

There is humility in baptism, and through Jesus's humility, He set an example for us to follow. Some faith traditions say He was also purifying the waters of baptism for all who follow in His footsteps. But Jesus's baptism also demonstrated His authority as God and displayed His relationship with the other two persons of the Trinity. At His baptism, all three are present: God the Son humbles Himself in the physical act of baptism, God the Spirit descends, and God the Father speaks. The scene is reminiscent of the roles each person of the Trinity plays in creation (see Genesis 1:1–3; John 1:1–3).

2. Read Psalm 2:7 and Isaiah 42:1. Then review Mark 1:11. How was this Old Testament language echoed at Jesus's baptism?

In this scene, Jesus's humility as Servant and His authority as Son are clear. And while a humble servant with divine authority seems to be a contradiction, in God's economy, it makes perfect sense. Jesus stepped fully into the juxtaposed roles, just as He was also both fully God and fully man (see John 1:14–18).

The book of Mark moves with urgency from one event to the next, and Mark tells us that immediately after Jesus's baptism, the Spirit drove Him to the wilderness where He was tempted.

3. Review 1:12–13.

Though the Spirit drove Jesus to the wilderness, the Spirit didn't tempt Him to sin: Satan did. And the Spirit didn't leave Him alone to struggle: The angels ministered to Him.

While Mark doesn't explain why Jesus went to the wilderness after His baptism, we do know that after high points in Jesus's ministry, He tended to retreat to places where He could be alone with His Father. Being publicly announced as the Son of God while in the waters of baptism would certainly count as a high point!

We also know that after milestones in our own walks of faith, we can be faced with strong temptations to sin. For Jesus, His time in the wilderness was both the aftermath of a high point *and* the preparation for public ministry. In these final days of preparation before Jesus's ministry began, there would've been nothing Satan would have loved more than to stop that ministry. But instead, Jesus's temptation likely served as preparation for what was to come—perhaps for Him, but also for us. God took what the enemy intended for evil and turned it around for our good. Because of what Jesus endured, He understands our joy, our grief, and our struggles firsthand. He faced temptations as we do, but as our perfect Savior, He overcame them.

4. Mark 1:14–15 is written below. **Circle the message Jesus proclaimed. Then underline the words He said.**

> Now after John was arrested, Jesus came into Galilee, proclaiming the gospel of God, and saying, "The time is fulfilled, and the kingdom of God is at hand; repent and believe in the gospel."

Jesus's ministry began when JTB, His forerunner, was taken away from the people. This short passage is easily overlooked, but it is absolutely vital in God's redemptive story. The gospel of God that Jesus proclaimed is *from* God and *about* God.

God's people had been waiting and longing and praying for God's kingdom to come, and Jesus told them that it (He) had finally arrived!

5. In Jesus's time, the people of Galilee were mostly working class and poor. They were also under the oppression of Roman rule. What would Jesus's message have meant to them?

6. What does it mean to you?

God's people wanted a king who would save them from their enemies and give them a peaceful life. But God had a plan that was infinitely more beautiful: He gave all of us a King who saves us from our sins and gives us eternal life. In Mark 1:15, the King Himself tells us our role: "Repent and believe in the gospel."

For Christians, when we repent of our sins and believe in the gospel, the one-time work of justification—being declared righteous because of Jesus's work—is complete. And the process of sanctification—becoming more like Jesus—is demonstrated through ongoing repentance and belief.

7. What things do you need to repent of?

8. What truths do you struggle to believe?

Mark 1:16–20

 **READ MARK 1:16–20**

As Jesus's ministry began, He called His first four disciples while they were working on the Sea of Galilee. The primary focus of Jesus's ministry was His teaching, and the common practice at the time was for potential students to be the ones to seek out a rabbi to teach them. But Jesus the Servant humbled Himself and sought *them* out. In ways they couldn't possibly have understood at the time, Jesus called the men not only to learn, but also to participate in an earthly mission of service and an eternal kingdom of glory!

1. How quickly did Simon and Andrew follow Jesus? Why is that important?

The disciples' response is important and sets an example that we would be wise to follow. But the main message here is Jesus's call.

2. **Review 1:17.** Write down the words Jesus said to Simon and Andrew:

In biblical times, children and teens almost always trained for the trade of their parents. Many people married in their early-to-mid teens and began their careers in the family business, preparing to take over as their parents aged. Simon, Andrew, James, and John likely all knew from the time they were young that they'd grow up to be fishermen. So Jesus didn't call them to be His disciples by telling them they were going to "plant seeds" like farmers or "heal the sick" like doctors. If He had, it's likely they would've felt unprepared or ill-equipped; He knew that in His perfect timing, He would equip them with all they needed. In His wisdom and kindness, He met these young fishermen where they were and called them using what they knew: fish.

3. **Read each of the passages below.** Match the Scripture reference with the fishing analogy.

Jeremiah 16:16	God catches Pharaoh (the dragon of the Nile) and casts him and his people (the fish) into the wilderness.
Ezekiel 29:1–5	The fishers are sent to catch sinful people and carry them to judgment.
Amos 4:1–3	Jesus wants His disciples to fish for people in order to bring them into God's Kingdom.
Mark 1:14–17	The women of Samaria who oppress the poor will be caught with fish hooks and led away by their enemies.

In the Old Testament, fishing analogies pointed to judgment and condemnation. But when Jesus fished, He brought good news and invited people into God's kingdom. He came to serve and to save.

4. Like most work, fishing isn't easy. It requires skill, patience, persistence, and even quiet. What does this tell you about the work Jesus called His disciples to?

5. What does this tell you about the work He's calling you to?

Mark 1:21–34

READ MARK 1:21–34

Three times a year, Jewish people went to Jerusalem to worship in the temple. But the rest of the year, they used smaller, local houses of worship called synagogues. Each synagogue had its own rabbis—teachers—who taught and led. Local rabbis would sometimes invite traveling rabbis or other locals to teach, which is how Jesus came to teach at the synagogue in Capernaum.

Though Mark doesn't tell us what Jesus taught in the synagogue, he does tell us how He taught: with authority.

1. **Look up *authority* (1:22) in a Greek lexicon.** What does it mean?

The people who heard Jesus knew there was something different about the way He spoke and taught. He embodied a position and a power that signified He had the right to speak for God. They were astonished. They didn't yet know what we know now: Jesus *is* God (see Colossians 1:19).

Jesus's primary ministry on earth was teaching, which He did with authority. His miracles and healings underscored that authority, like we see with the unclean spirit.

2. **Review 1:23–27.** Where is Jesus's authority present?

The unclean spirit—or demon—knew who Jesus was. And Jesus didn't need objects, formulas, or special prayers to cast it out; He used His authority and His voice. Satan fights against all of God's good and holy plans, and Jesus was the pinnacle of His great plan for mankind, so it's no surprise that Jesus faced the demonic in His ministry. Jesus cast out demons a number of times in the Gospels, and though they often fought back, He always had the victory. These individual victories point us toward His ultimate victory through the cross.

3. **Read Colossians 2:15 in the ESV, NIV, and NLT.** What did Jesus's death and resurrection do to the spiritual rulers and authorities?

After the accounts of Jesus teaching and casting out a demon, we read the first account of healing in the book of Mark. Each healing recorded in the Gospels is different: Sometimes Jesus touches people, sometimes He speaks, sometimes He directs them to an action, and sometimes He doesn't even see them in person. Our creative God made every person unique, and His loving Son served every person with unique care. In Mark 1:31, Jesus went to Simon's mother-in-law, someone He probably knew well, and "took her by the hand and lifted her up."

4. What did Simon's mother-in-law do after she was healed?

Simon's mother-in-law lived with Simon and Andrew, and it's very likely that when He was in Capernaum, Jesus also lived with them. While healing her, Jesus went into a part of the house that only household members were allowed to enter. So while we don't know exactly how she served them, we see gratitude as her immediate response. Because of the great thing Jesus had done for her, she served Him and His people.

Already, people were in awe of Jesus. Word about Him had spread, and as soon as the Sabbath was over, the "whole city" (v. 33) gathered at His door, waiting to be freed from demons or healed from sickness. It only took a short while for the people to believe Jesus had authority to heal them. And it's only taken a few verses of the book of Mark for us to see Jesus's ultimate authority over all things.

5. **Review the passages below.** Beside each Scripture reference, write what Jesus demonstrated His authority over: demons, sickness, or people.

- Mark 1:17 _____

- Mark 1:25 _____

- Mark 1:31 _____

DAY 5

Mark 1:35–45

 **READ MARK 1:35–45**

Today's reading started with Jesus rising before the sun to spend time alone in prayer.

1. If intentional solo prayer was vital for Jesus, what does that tell you about your need for prayer?

2. Do you have a routine for prayer? If so, describe it below. If not, describe what you'd like your prayer life to look like.

By the time the disciples woke up, a crowd was looking for Jesus. The disciples tracked Him down and tried to nudge Him along to appease the miracle seekers. But Jesus had clarity and certainty about what He needed to do next: keep moving and keep teaching—His plan was to go beyond

Capernaum to the other cities in the Galilee region. Jesus made His Father's plan His priority, even though it wasn't the decision the people wanted.

The people of Capernaum may have been interested in Jesus only as a miracle worker, but His main ministry was teaching. We can't diminish the importance of His miracles to that ministry, however. After all, exorcisms demonstrated His authority over sin and Satan, pointing to their eventual defeat. And healings demonstrated His authority over sickness and death, pointing to the eventual restoration of creation. Jesus's miracles supported and confirmed His message.

3. **Read 1:14–15.** What was Jesus's message?

Jesus and His disciples traveled through the Galilee region—an area in northern Israel made up of more than two hundred small towns. Mark tells us He preached in their synagogues and—underscoring His message—drove out demons.

During this time, Jesus also healed. *Leprosy* was a term used to describe a wide range of skin disorders as we know them today, from psoriasis to ringworm. After the exodus, God gave His people specific instructions concerning these disorders and diseases.

4. **Read Leviticus 13:45–46.** What did people suffering from leprosy have to do?

Cleanliness laws were given to prevent the spread of disease, and they were ultimately for the good of God's people, but this doesn't make the afflicted person's reality any less heartbreaking. People with leprosy were isolated religiously—unable to worship with God's people; they were isolated socially—unable to eat and dance with their communities; and they were isolated financially—unable to work for a living. Not only did they feel agonizing physical pain, but they suffered emotionally as well.

When the man with leprosy came to Jesus, his desperation was obvious. He knelt before Jesus and implored Him, "If you will, you can make me clean" (1:40). The man knew Jesus could heal him; his question was whether Jesus *would*. The suffering man believed in God's power, even though he was uncertain about His compassion. But Jesus, always compassionate, was moved with pity.

5. Read Leviticus 13:45–46, then review Mark 1:41. What did Jesus do and say? According to the laws in Leviticus, why was this radical?

Jesus could've healed the man with only His voice, but the man needed physical *and* emotional healing, and Jesus touched him. The man with leprosy didn't make Jesus unclean. Instead, Jesus made him clean.

Jesus reminds the man to follow God's law by going to the priest and offering sacrifices, and He also tells the man something strange: not to tell anyone about what happened. We'll see throughout the Gospels that He had different commands for Jews and Gentiles (that is, any non-Jewish person) when He healed them. For the Gentiles, He often allowed and even encouraged them to tell others about what He did for them. But within Jewish communities where He healed people, He usually told them to keep quiet.

Jesus wasn't contradicting Himself. This is referred to as the "messianic secret"—Jesus's plan to keep His identity as the Messiah concealed among the Jews until the right time. This is one of the reasons Jesus instructed people not to tell about what He'd done for them. As we know, He also didn't want people seeking Him as *only* a healer or miracle worker—He wanted people seeking Him because of who He was and the message He taught. But since Jesus's message seemed like a threat to both Jewish and Roman leaders, it's likely He didn't want word about Him spreading too quickly. In His own words, His "hour [had] not yet come" (John 2:4).

Of course, Jesus knew that the man wouldn't be able to keep the miracle to himself. And as the man told people, even more of them came to Him in search of healing.

6. What has God done for you that is too wonderful for you to keep to yourself?

Whatever your story, if you know Christ, you know that He has done something wonderful for you. He's the miracle. He's the good news. And He's where the joy is!

7. What stood out to you most in this week's study? Why?

8. What did you learn or relearn about God and His character this week?

Corresponding Psalm & Prayer

 **READ PSALM 85**

1. What correlation do you see between Psalm 85 and this week's study of Jesus and His kingdom?

2. What portions of this psalm stand out to you most?

3. Close by praying this prayer aloud:

Father,
  I praise You for who You are. You are the God who restores and revives! You are the God who grants repentance and brings new life! Righteousness goes before You.

Father, I have sinned, and I appeal to Your mercy. I repent of my sins and turn to You and ask You to make my heart clean. Like the people in Capernaum, I confess that sometimes I'm interested only in what You can do for me, not in who You are. Yet You have still served me despite the ways I don't value You above all else. I repent of not loving You well in my thoughts and actions.

Show me Your steadfast love, O Lord. Revive and restore me. Help me not turn back to folly. Keep my feet steady on the path of righteousness. Turn me from my selfishness and make me look more like Your Son, Jesus, who had a heart to serve others.

I surrender my life to You, Lord—every moment of my day, each decision I make, I yield my will and way to Your perfect will and way.

I love You too. Amen.

DAY 7

Rest, Catch Up,
or Dig Deeper

 WEEKLY CHALLENGE

In Mark 1:35, Jesus made time to pray by getting up while it was still dark. Making intentional time to pray is important for a growing relationship with God, and it will likely require some sacrifice—whether it's getting up early, staying up late, silencing your phone, using your kids' nap time, or getting away during your lunch break at school or work. This week, choose and commit to a daily intentional block of time for prayer. It may vary in time of day or length from day to day, but mark it on your calendar so it doesn't get lost in your schedule. Keep a prayer journal and take note not only of your prayers, but also of what God is doing in your heart through this time.

─ Scripture to Memorize ─

"But it shall not be so among you. But whoever would be great among you must be your servant, and whoever would be first among you must be slave of all."

Mark 10:43–44

Mark 2–3:
The News of the Servant

DAILY BIBLE READING

Day 1: Mark 2:1–17
Day 2: Mark 2:18–28
Day 3: Mark 3:1–12
Day 4: Mark 3:13–21
Day 5: Mark 3:22–35
Day 6: Psalm 37
Day 7: Catch-Up Day

Corresponds to Days 280 and 282 of *The Bible Recap.*

WEEKLY CHALLENGE

See page 64 for more information.

Mark 2:1–17

 **READ MARK 2:1-17**

If a daily newspaper circulated in ancient Israel, no doubt Jesus would have made the headlines. The news of His miracles spread rapidly throughout Galilee, and the people were amazed by His power to heal, cast out demons, and preach with authority.

Four friends heard these stories and really believed Jesus had the power to make their paralyzed friend walk. So they devised a plan to take him to Jesus.

1. What was their dilemma when they arrived at Jesus's home in Capernaum?

2. What was their remedy?

3. What does their plan say about their belief in Jesus?

It's no wonder that while He was preaching, His home in Capernaum was crowded by those who were seeking a cure or even just curious about Him. But the quartet of friends was determined. They climbed up to the thatched roof, removed some roof panels, hauled their friend up to the roof somehow, and lowered him down in the midst of the crowd. This plan required a lot of work. These faith-filled friends must have truly believed their friend would be healed!

4. Beyond Jesus's ability to heal, what abilities do 2:5 and 2:8 reveal?

Jesus saw the men's faith and perceived the scribes' questioning. The divine Son of Man had eyes to see the depths of their hearts. Jesus could have immediately wowed the crowd with another big miracle, but He chose to first address the broken man's heart. Unrestored legs wouldn't keep him out of the kingdom, but an unrestored heart certainly would. With an abundance of kindness, Jesus addressed the man's greatest need by forgiving his sins.

All those who stood by were likely shocked by Jesus's words. Imagine the friends' momentary defeat at Jesus's first words, "Son, your sins are forgiven." Picture them watching from a bird's-eye view—looking down through the hole in the roof—wanting to shout, "Jesus, we brought him to You to fix his legs! We didn't carry him all this way because of sin!" And take note of the scribes' response to Jesus's statement—they accused Him of blasphemy.

5. **Use a Bible dictionary or other Bible tool to define** *blasphemy.*

The scribes were correct in thinking, *Only God can forgive sins*, but they were unwilling to believe that Jesus *is* God. Jesus displayed His divinity through His authority over sin and His power to heal, but they wouldn't believe. Jesus gave simple instructions to the man on the mat, and he immediately walked out the door—just as his four friends had hoped.

6. Mark 2:12 says the crowds "were all amazed and glorified God, saying, 'We never saw anything like this!'" Describe a time when you were amazed by God's intervention, and write a simple prayer of praise.

After this healing, Jesus left His home and walked along the sea. The crowds followed Him, and He seized the opportunity to continue teaching. When Jesus passed by Levi (also known as Matthew) the tax collector, He invited the man to follow Him.

Matthew followed Jesus immediately, and his yes was a radical one. Tax collectors were hated by their fellow Jews because they chose to partner with the enemy, the Roman Empire. They stole from their own Jewish communities to build the kingdom of their oppressor and fill their own pockets. Matthew was no exception to this job description. His tax booth by the sea meant he probably took advantage of the very fishermen he would follow Jesus alongside. His yes to Jesus burned bridges with his employer, Rome. There would be no return to his lavish income. Yet in spite of being despised by the Jews he took advantage of, he believed following Jesus was the better reward.

7. Review 2:15–16. The phrase *tax collectors and sinners* is mentioned three times in these two verses. Use a Bible commentary to describe what the occupation of tax collector entailed and what "sinner" meant.

8. What are a few modern-day comparisons to a tax collector and a "sinner"?

These people, who were considered outcasts by the religious leaders, were reclining with the only One who had never sinned. Jesus wasn't afraid of becoming *like* them, nor was He afraid to be *near* them. He reclined at a table alongside them—a posture reserved for personal friendship. Jesus had all the information about their condition, and He had complete authority over each of them, yet He served them in friendship. They didn't have a true understanding of God, but God Himself drew near to them in love.

9. Recall the moment when you became aware of your need for the spiritual healing only Jesus can provide. Write a few sentences describing how God transformed you from sinner to righteous.

10. Now that you've been made spiritually well, how can you share hope and truth with people who need spiritual wellness?

DAY 2

Mark 2:18–28

 **READ MARK 2:18-28**

In today's passage, the Pharisees and JTB's disciples were fasting, but Jesus and His disciples weren't. Some from the crowd asked Jesus, "Why don't your disciples do things like the others do?" As He often did, He replied to their question with a question of His own.

1. **Review 2:19–20.** What title did Jesus assign Himself?

2. **Read Isaiah 62:5 and Hosea 2:16, 19–20.** What similar language is found in these Old Testament passages? Using a Bible study tool, describe the significance of this title.

Jesus didn't pull this analogy out of thin air. In ancient Israel, many rabbis declared that during a weeklong wedding celebration, *joy* was more important than observing religious laws. And some rabbis would even go as far as saying that if a law got in the way of joy during wedding festivities, you didn't have to keep it! Jesus's choice of illustration communicated this idea: *I'm not the Pharisees or JTB—I'm the bridegroom and the festivities are happening now. And, wherever I am, the joy that accompanies weddings is. I'm where the joy is!*

Next, Jesus spoke to the crowd like a tailor or a vineyard owner. The kingdom of God isn't just a patch over the law of Moses or Jewish tradition—Jesus came to create something new, not patch something old. The arrival of the Messiah ushered in a new era with new ways. His analogies signified that following Him would look different from their long-held traditions.

3. Take a survey of your religious and personal practices. Do you have any traditions or routines that may hold too high a position in your life?

Many knew that Jesus and His disciples were not fasting according to certain standards, but on one Sabbath day, when the disciples broke off heads of grain, the Pharisees were outraged that Jesus and His followers were harvesting on the Sabbath.

4. **Review 2:25–26. Read Deuteronomy 23:25 and 1 Samuel 21:1–6.** What actions were permitted according to Old Testament law?

Jesus's question "Have you never read . . . ?" was a pointed one. *Of course they had!* This would be akin to asking a jockey if he'd ever heard of a horse. The Pharisees prided themselves on knowing Scripture. They'd read it and even memorized it, but they didn't fully understand it. They focused on the law and missed the heart behind the law.

Jesus's question to the Pharisees highlighted the growing tension between His mission and their rigid rule keeping. Jesus never violated God's commands regarding the Sabbath, and He never encouraged His disciples to do so. He did, however, break man-made laws to push back the oppressive religious regime and demonstrate that their traditions weren't God's laws.

According to Deuteronomy 23:25, the law declared that heads of grain could be plucked as you were walking along the way. And in 1 Samuel 21:1–6, even David was permitted to eat the bread of the Presence and share it with his men because there was great need among them. Jesus corrected the Pharisees as He pointed out: "The Sabbath was made to *bless* you and you've made it a burden to everyone by adding your own laws and elevating them to the level of God's laws."

5. Read Genesis 2:1–3. Describe the heart of God as it relates to Sabbath rest. Use a Bible study tool if it's helpful.

6. Why is resting necessary for the Christ-follower today?

Resting predated the law. Resting occurred on the seventh day of creation after the triune God (Father, Son, and Spirit) created *everything*. The seventh day is a holy day—a blessed ("happy") day—and it was created for man to bless him. God wants to bless His kids. He knows we're tired! He knows we need true rest in Him. "The Sabbath was made for man, not man for the Sabbath" (Mark 2:27). Sabbath rest provides opportunities for God's kids to release their hand from the plow, to cease trying to control everything, and to trust that the Maker of heaven and earth is in control.

7. What things do you need to release control of? List them below, then pray a prayer of repentance. Thank God for being a good Father who is in control.

8. **Review 2:28, and read Daniel 7:13. Use a Greek lexicon to look up the word *lord*.** What is the significance of Jesus calling Himself "Son of Man"?

Jesus closed His reply to the religious leaders by making one bold final statement. He called Himself the "Son of Man," a blatant announcement that He is the Messiah foretold by Old Testament prophets. This statement was a declaration of His deity. He added that He is the lord—the master—of the Sabbath. The Son of Man was there on the seventh day when rest was instituted. And the One who instituted the Sabbath knew His finished work on the cross is the only way for God's kids to have complete rest.

9. In what areas of your life (even your thought life) do you need to rest in the truth of what Jesus has accomplished for you?

10. Are there any practical steps you need to take to make that more of a reality in your life?

Mark 3:1–12

 **READ MARK 3:1–12**

Jesus, a law-abiding Jew with reverence for His Father, went to the synagogue on the Sabbath day. Inside, He noticed a man with a withered hand. This would've been an unusual encounter because people with disabilities weren't allowed in the synagogue at the time. It's almost certain this man had been manipulated by the Pharisees and used as a plant to trap Jesus. They were relentless in their efforts to take out their enemy. Jesus accurately read the situation and leaned in to demonstrate not only love for God but love for the man with the withered hand.

1. In your own words, summarize why the Pharisees were repeatedly critical of Jesus. **Refer to yesterday's reading or a Bible study tool if it's helpful.**

The Pharisees devoted their lives to being set apart for God, and they were set on defending the laws of God, even if the "laws of God" were laws they created themselves. Not long before this, Jesus had announced that He is "lord of the Sabbath," a phrase that understandably enraged them. They continued gathering information about Him, but despite all His miracles, they refused to believe His account of who He was.

Jesus continued to reveal God's heart to them through His questions. Notice the phrasing of His question in 3:4. According to the Pharisees' Sabbath traditions, if a man cut his finger on the Sabbath, he could stop the bleeding but he couldn't put ointment on it. He could stop it from getting worse but he couldn't make it better. Jesus could've healed this man's hand on any day of the week, but by choosing to do it on the Sabbath, He made a point to the hard-hearted religious elite that there is never a wrong day to do something good.

2. Review 3:5. What two emotions did Jesus have at the same time?

3. Do these two emotions seem conflicting? Why or why not?

The Son of Man was angered by their opposition and grieved by the state of their hearts. Many of us have been taught we shouldn't be angry, but Scripture never says that.

4. Read Ephesians 4:26. What does it instruct us to avoid?

In the Gospels, we find several examples of Jesus being angry—and for very good reason.

5. Read the text and match the reasons for Jesus's righteous anger.

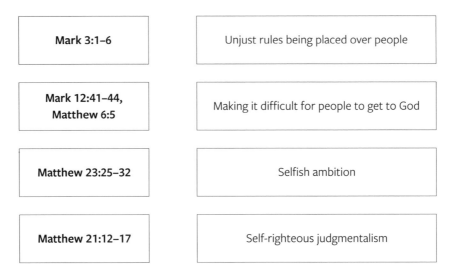

Mark 3:1–6	Unjust rules being placed over people
Mark 12:41–44, Matthew 6:5	Making it difficult for people to get to God
Matthew 23:25–32	Selfish ambition
Matthew 21:12–17	Self-righteous judgmentalism

6. Read Genesis 6:6 and Isaiah 63:10. What emotion did God express?

7. Look up that word in a Bible dictionary or Hebrew lexicon and write down what you find.

Jesus's righteous anger and grieving heart mirrored the Father and the Holy Spirit during moments when His people acted unrighteously. The humble, servant-hearted Savior held His anger and sadness simultaneously while dismissing His enemies' false accusations. Jesus served the "least of these" by pushing back against the unjust, ungodly religious systems that oppressed them.

8. What is your typical response when you're angry?

9. How can you mimic Jesus's reaction when you're angry?

10. What things stir your righteous anger, and what causes you to be grieved?

11. Review 3:7–12. On the map below, circle the cities mentioned in the passage. Using the key, note each city's distance from Capernaum.

Figure 2.1

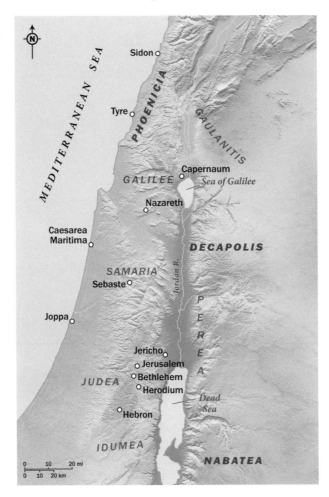

City/Region	Distance (approximate)
Galilee	
Judea	
Jerusalem	
Idumea	
Tyre	
Sidon	

A twenty-mile walk would take roughly one day. As the map shows, people came from all directions, sometimes walking for days or weeks round trip, to be near Jesus. The Son of Man's popularity was growing, and He and the disciples found it more difficult to control the crowds. While the crowds continued gathering, Jesus developed a brilliant plan, instructing His disciples to get a boat so He could anchor offshore. The distance from the crowd kept Him from being crushed, and His voice carried over the water like a natural microphone. Jesus continued preaching the good news, healing those who were sick, and casting out demons.

12. What statement did the demons make about Jesus?

13. Why do you think Jesus responded to them the way He did?

The unclean spirits rightly acknowledged His position as Son of God, but even though their words were true, Jesus commanded them to be silent. Jesus wanted to be known as the Son of God, but not via the malicious intent of evil spirits who weren't concerned about His timing or plan. His true identity as the servant Savior, the long-awaited Messiah, would be revealed through His righteous words and works and in the Father's perfect time.

14. Take a moment to reflect on Jesus's title "Son of God" and what it means that He has chosen to reveal Himself to you. Write a short prayer of gratitude thanking Him for making His true identity known to you.

Mark 3:13–21

 **READ MARK 3:13–21**

At the end of a long day of ministry Jesus left the boat where He had been ministering and walked up a mountain. Luke's gospel gives us more information about this moment, describing how Jesus spent the night praying, and when the sun came up, He gathered all the disciples who had been following Him and chose twelve to be His apostles.

1. **Use a Bible dictionary or study tool to define the words *disciple* and *apostle*.**

2. What is the primary difference between these two words?

The word *disciple* (*mathētēs*) means "learner" or "follower." An *apostle* (*apostolos*) is one who is a messenger, sent on a mission. Jesus called these twelve young men—most of whom were probably teenagers—to have a deeper look into His life and to gain a deeper understanding of

His message and ministry. Essentially, Jesus was saying, "Come and see! And soon you'll go and tell!"

3. **Use a study Bible or other study tool to note the similarities and differences among the twelve apostles Jesus chose.** What might be their strengths? What might be their weaknesses? Record all the information you can.

This carefully selected crew of twelve would eventually turn the world upside down. Among them were a denier, a betrayer, a deceiver, a doubter, and a religious fanatic. There were likely practical skills that each apostle brought to the table, benefitting the mission. The fishermen were well-versed in boating, the tax collector likely had advanced numerical ability and attention to detail. Despite their perceived strengths and weaknesses, Jesus saw them for who they were, and He knew who they would become once they yielded to Him and committed to His Father's will.

4. **Read Matthew 28:16–20 and Romans 1:1–6.** What is the difference between a disciple and an apostle?

Though Mark intentionally used *apostle* and *disciple* to differentiate two types of Christ-followers, some say there's evidence in Scripture that if we are in Christ, we are both. Even now, Jesus calls us to follow Him *and* He sends us out to be messengers of the good news unto the ends of the earth.

5. How does being a follower and a messenger of Jesus shape your daily life? How often are you aware that you have these positions?

6. What does it mean to you that God chose *you* to be one of His followers, despite your sins and weaknesses?

Today's reading ends with another description of the crowd's magnitude. There were so many people at Jesus's house when He returned home that their daily life was disrupted—they couldn't even eat! When Jesus's family heard all that was going on, they accused Him of being out of His mind.

7. Have you ever been misunderstood or accused by those you love? If so, briefly describe what happened.

8. What was your immediate response?

Tomorrow, and throughout the rest of this study, we'll dive deeper into how Jesus never let man's opinions deter Him from His Father's mission and how He instructed His followers, like us, to do the same.

God, help us to be a people who remain faithful to do Your will even in the face of opposition.

Mark 3:22–35

  READ MARK 3:22-35

While Jesus continued teaching at His house, the scribes heckled the crowd, making strong statements about Him. In yesterday's reading, we saw Jesus remain steadfast to His mission despite growing opposition. Today we saw the religious leaders attempt to dissuade the crowds from believing in Jesus's true messianic identity and cause them to associate Him with a different authority instead.

1. Who is Beelzebul? **Use a Bible study tool to help you choose all answers that apply.**

    A. another name for demons

    B. a name for Satan or the devil

    C. a name meaning "lord of mosquitos"

    D. a name meaning "lord of the flies"

    E. a name for the ghost of Nebuchadnezzar

    F. a name meaning "lord of dung"

Baal-zebub was a Philistine god worshiped at Ekron whose name literally means "lord of the flies." You can read about him in 2 Kings 1:2–6. Pagans believed Baal-zebub had the authority to dispel flies, which were a source of sickness. Over time, the Jews changed the name "Baal-zebub" to "Baal-zebul," which means "lord of the dung" and is a title of utmost contempt. They assigned this name to Satan himself as a means of declaring how abhorrent he is.*

---

*"G954 - beelzeboul – Strong's Greek Lexicon (net)," Blue Letter Bible, accessed 22 January, 2024. https://www.blueletterbible.org/lexicon/g954/net/mgnt/0-1/.

When the scribes stepped onto the scene and claimed Jesus was practicing under the authority of Beelzebul, they were making a vicious and cynical attack on Him. This public accusation was a big deal. In their religious minds, Jesus had already broken too many rules and had gone too far, but before they could destroy Him, they needed to discredit Him among the crowds who were in awe of Him.

2. **Summarize Jesus's response in 3:24–27.** What point did Jesus make?

Essentially, Jesus stated: "I'm not working for Satan—I'm defeating him. Satan is strong but I'm stronger." And as One who has authority, Jesus warned His accusers of the danger they were in by attributing God's power and purpose to the enemy.

3. Based on your current understanding, explain Jesus's statement that "whoever blasphemes against the Holy Spirit never has forgiveness, but is guilty of an eternal sin" in the space below. Feel free to use a Bible study tool to gain a deeper understanding.

In this text and in the other synoptic gospels (Matthew 12:22–37, Luke 11:14–23), "blasphemy against the Holy Spirit" seems to point to how the Pharisees persistently and arrogantly attributed God's work to Satan when they knew the accusation was false. They weren't just calling Him a demon; they were denying His deity.

Perhaps blasphemy of the Holy Spirit is specifically this type of incident—attributing the Holy Spirit's work to Satan. Mark makes it plain in other areas of his gospel that forgiveness through repentance is always possible. This sin isn't "too big" for God to forgive—instead, this is a sin that prevents pardon because it signifies a lack of repentance. Only a willful heart, turned far from Him, would attribute to the devil what is blatantly Divine.

4. Have you ever been concerned that any of your sins were too big to forgive?

5. Read 1 John 1:9. How does this shape your view of sin and God's ability to forgive?

After this big moment, Mary and Jesus's brothers called for Him. The crowds passed the news to Jesus: "Your mother and your brothers are outside, seeking you." But Jesus remained focused on the mission of His Father and used it as a teaching moment. He asked, "Who are my mother and my brothers?"

6. What point was Jesus making about biological family?

7. How was this statement countercultural?

Jesus knew His mother and brothers. He hadn't tossed them aside, and He didn't forget their existence once His ministry began. In Jewish culture, the family was the building block of society. In fact, there's a Hebrew saying that goes, "The family is the first essential cell of human society." Jews viewed family as a gift from God and the most important thing other than God. When Jesus made this statement, "Whoever does the will of God, he is my brother and sister and mother," He wasn't diminishing His biological family. Instead, He was elevating the importance of family within the kingdom of God—Jews and Gentiles of every nation, tribe, and tongue.

8. **Read Hebrews 12:5–6 and Romans 8:16–17.** How is your heart stirred with affection for the Father, knowing He calls you His child? What peace is found knowing you are a coheir with Christ?

9. What stood out to you most in this week's study? Why?

10. What did you learn or relearn about God and His character this week?

DAY 6

Corresponding Psalm & Prayer

 **READ PSALM 37**

1. What correlation do you see between Psalm 37 and this week's study of Jesus and His kingdom?

2. What portions of this psalm stand out to you most?

3. Close by praying this prayer aloud:

> *Father,*
>   *You are a righteous God. Thank You that in Your perfect timing, You will bring justice to the wicked. You know the lies the enemy tells*

about You and about me—just like he told lies about Your Son, Jesus. And You can be trusted to bring the truth to light in the long run.

I confess that my mind can often be consumed by things that don't glorify You—things like my reputation, fear about the future, selfish anger, and the desire for control. I repent of my sins and turn to You; only You can make my heart clean.

Kill off my anxious spinning, God. Uproot my sinful thoughts and desires. Help me to delight in You. Help me to trust that You are working on my behalf. Help me to be still and wait patiently for You to act. Help me to do good and befriend faithfulness. As a member of Your family, help me to do Your will. And thank You for the opportunity to be a part of the only eternal mission: life in Your kingdom!

I surrender my life to You, Lord—every moment of my day, each decision I make, I yield my will and way to Your perfect will and way.

I love You too. Amen.

Rest, Catch Up, or Dig Deeper

WEEKLY CHALLENGE

In Mark 2:27, Jesus said, "The Sabbath was made for man, not man for the Sabbath." In modern culture, the ideas rooted in Sabbath are often misunderstood, and most of us don't set aside a full twenty-four-hour period each week to cease from work, errands, and accomplishments in order to rest in the Lord and deepen our time with our community. Today, look at your schedule for the rest of the month and aim to carve out one day each week to practice the Sabbath. (By the way, "practice" implies that you haven't perfected it yet, so don't expect to be able to fully make the mental or practical shifts into Sabbath mode if you're new to this spiritual discipline.) If you need more help understanding what a Sabbath practice looks like, check out MyDGroup.org/Resources/Mark for additional resources. And while our focus in this study is on the ways Jesus demonstrated *service*, it's helpful to remember that serving and Sabbath work together—you can't pour from an empty cup.

— Scripture to Memorize —

"For even the Son of Man
came not to be served but
to serve, and to give his life
as a ransom for many."

Mark 10:45

Mark 4–5:
The Greatness
of the Servant

DAILY BIBLE READING

Day 1: Mark 4:1–20

Day 2: Mark 4:21–34

Day 3: Mark 4:35–41

Day 4: Mark 5:1–20

Day 5: Mark 5:21–43

Day 6: Psalm 29

Day 7: Catch-Up Day

Corresponds to Day 288 of *The Bible Recap*.

WEEKLY CHALLENGE

See page 91 for more information.

Mark 4:1–20

 **READ MARK 4:1-20**

Once again in His floating pulpit on the Sea of Galilee, Jesus preached to a crowd using water as nature's microphone. Each person on the shoreline had a reason for being there—some had a genuine excitement that He may be the promised Messiah, others had idle curiosity, and still others had contempt for Jesus, looking only for a way to trip Him up. Knowing each of their motivations, Jesus spoke in parables so that those who were willing to lean in could better understand His message of the kingdom.

1. **Using a Greek lexicon or Bible dictionary, look up the word *parable*.** Describe it in your own words.

After urging them to not just hear, but *listen*, He told a parable about a sower spreading seed in different locations. This was a straightforward story for a group of people whose lives revolved around agriculture.

The familiar, everyday examples Jesus used would've been like saying, "The ice cream in the freezer stayed cold, the ice cream in the refrigerator softened, the ice cream on the counter melted, and the ice cream in the sun spoiled." It might have seemed like He was simply stating the obvious, so it's possible that many only heard it at face value and missed His point.

2. Do you ever catch yourself skimming the Scriptures or zoning out during a sermon because you assume you already know the information? What does this reveal about your attitude toward truth?

The disinterested probably thought this was a story about farming methods, a warning about birds, or even an agricultural get-rich-quick idea. And Jesus left the crowd before giving them the key. But those who were hungry for the truth of the kingdom leaned into His parable and asked Him more questions, which helped unlock their understanding of the kingdom. He reiterated that only those with ears to hear *would* hear. Jesus explained to His curious disciples the purpose of His speaking in parables by quoting Isaiah 6:9–10.

3. Using a Bible study tool, explain the differences between the following words Jesus used in verse 12:

- see / perceive: _____

  _____

- hear / understand: _____

  _____

Jesus made the point that everyone hearing His parables had two options: They could lean in and hear the truth, or turn a deaf ear and miss it. The key to understanding the kingdom parallel was found in what the "seed" represented.

4. Review 4:14. What was the sower spreading?

5. With that in mind, what does the soil represent?

6. Match the type of soil to the type of heart that the Word landed on:

The path	A heart that seems eager for the Word, but is shallow and rooted in something other than truth; it crumbles in trials or persecution
Rocky soil	A heart that truly receives the Word but is less interested in truth than the instant gratification of a fallen world; it is unfruitful
Thorny soil	A heart that is transformed by the truth of the Word; it spreads the truth to as many people as will listen
Good soil	A heart that is hardened to the Word and unable to hear the truth

7. What is the threat to the seed on the rocky soil?

8. What is the threat to the seed on the thorny soil?

9. Take a moment to reflect. What kind of soil best represents your heart right now?

10. If it's the path, the rocky ground, or the thorny ground, write out a short prayer asking God to soften your heart.

In His great generosity, the Sower sends out the seed to all types of soil, giving every spot of ground a chance to receive the truth. And God, the Maker of the soil, is the one who can soften our hearts to receive the truth.

It's worth noting that both trials (rocky ground) and abundance (thorns) can choke out the truth in our lives. We may pray for lives of ease, but without trials, we forget that we need to rely on God. We may face challenges, but without the relief that comes from knowing and trusting God, we will despair. But where the truth falls on soft hearts ready to receive, the gospel perseveres and bears fruit beyond our greatest imagination!

Mark 4:21–34

READ MARK 4:21-34

We learned yesterday that Jesus spoke in parables to explain the kingdom to those who were willing to lean in, so it makes sense that today's reading requires some serious leaning in. Every parable has a key to understanding the deeper truth, and today's key piggybacks off the parable of the sower. The conclusion of yesterday's parable was that the Word of God is sown, and in good soil its truth produces an abundant harvest of spiritual fruit. Let's keep that key in mind as we lean in.

1. Review 4:21. Why wouldn't someone put an open-flame lamp under a basket or a bed?

2. What's the practical purpose of a lamp?

3. What do you think the lamp represents in this parable?

If you've ever been to a candlelight Christmas Eve service, you've seen a visual representation of the responsibility truth bearers have. One person lights a candle, then one by one, they pass the fire along until the whole room is holding a flame. As each candle is lit, the space grows brighter, pushing out the darkness.

This is a picture of how the kingdom of God advances. Someone who receives the Word is transformed by the truth and passes it on to another, who passes it on to another. A lamp isn't meant to be hidden—its very purpose is to dispel the darkness. Likewise, the gospel of Christ is meant to be spoken and shared to drive out the darkness of our fallen world with His light.

In 4:23–25 Jesus reminded those who had been given the truth to not become passive, but to lean in all the more. Essentially, He said, "The more you put into this, the more you're going to get out of it."

4. Have you ever experienced the momentum of spiritual growth that led to better habits, which led to more spiritual growth? Describe it.

It's easy to misunderstand 4:25 as God taking the truth away from people—it isn't a punishment; it's a warning. Think of it this way: If your heart is receiving the seed (that is, the Word) in good soil, your life will bear fruit; and if your life is bearing fruit, you will also have the seeds *inside* that fruit so that more seeds can be planted and more fruit can grow! But if your heart is receiving the Word on the path, rocks, or thorns, you won't even have those initial seeds for very long. With no seeds, you have no fruit; and with no fire, you have no light.

Jesus's next parable built on the first two.

5. Review 4:26–29. In your own words, summarize what Jesus said about the kingdom.

Agriculture was the center of life for Jesus's audience. They knew that if you put a seed in the ground and the conditions were favorable, it would grow into maturity and be fruitful. But the scientific process underneath it all was largely a mystery to them. Likewise, Jesus said that the kingdom of God was a mystery to human understanding. They may not have been able to see *how* the growth was happening in the soil of life, but Jesus assured them that through His Word, it was.

6. Read Isaiah 55:11. What does it say about the Word of God?

7. How does that apply to this parable?

We can't always see what's happening in our hearts during our own spiritual growth. But as it overflows into fruitful action, the result is unmistakable. It's incredible that God invites us to be the bearers of spiritual fruit that feeds others!

8. Think of people you know personally whose spiritual lives you admire. What kind of spiritual fruit have you seen growing in their lives?

Jesus's last parable in today's reading is well-known to many believers, but hopefully, in the context of the previous three parables, you'll understand this one in a new way!

9. Review 4:30–32. In your own words, summarize Jesus's statements about the kingdom of God.

When it comes to the kingdom of God, looks can be deceiving. Like the flame, the harvest, and the mustard seed, the kingdom is growing and will continue to grow. Don't be discouraged if you fail to see fruit growing as quickly as you'd like in your own life or the lives of others—growth takes time. And God promises that He is doing it!

In 4:33, Mark used this phrase to describe Jesus's audience: "as they were able to hear it." His words are a challenge to humble ourselves and admit we don't have it all figured out. This serves as a reminder to lean in and look for truth in God's Word. When we do that, God steps in, opens our eyes and ears, and equips us to bear His fruit and to see His kingdom grow.

Although Jesus spoke publicly in parables, 4:34 tells us that He always explained them to His disciples. That was His plan all along—His disciples would make disciple-making disciples. And just as a sanctuary on Christmas Eve lights up with each lit candle, the truth of the kingdom was spread from those twelve around the world. And now it's our turn to pass the flame!

10. In what relationships do you need to "pass the flame" of the gospel? Write out a prayer asking God to open a door for that conversation this week! If no one comes to mind, write out a prayer asking God to bring at least one person to mind today.

Mark 4:35–41

READ MARK 4:35–41

To set the stage for what Jesus does in today's reading, it's important to understand the setting. The Sea of Galilee is the lowest freshwater lake on earth with its surface almost 700 feet below sea level. It's surrounded by hills and cliffs, giving it unique and unpredictable weather patterns.

1. Do a web search for the Sea of Galilee and fill in the blanks on the map below:

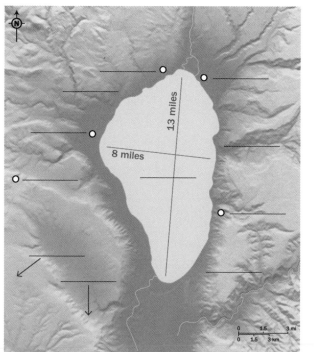

- Bethsaida
- Cana
- Capernaum
- Feeding 5,000
- Gentile Region
- Gerasenes
- Jerusalem
- Magdala
- Nazareth
- Sea of Galilee
- Sermon on the Mount

Jesus had a long day of ministry, but instead of heading back to the shore after teaching from the boat, He told His disciples they were all headed from the west side of the lake (the Jewish side) to the east side (the Gentile side)—away from the crowds.

Historians estimate that their small vessel was approximately seven feet wide by twenty-five feet long—leaving room for about fifteen grown men. The sides of the boat were roughly four feet tall. So when a violent windstorm suddenly struck (v. 37), the waves had to be at least four feet high to break over the edges! This was not a normal storm but a *massive* one. It was so big, in fact, that even these seasoned fishermen were terrified for their lives. Yet the disciples found Jesus asleep.

2. How would you feel if you were a disciple in that boat?

Jesus's disciples experienced a very normal fear of death, followed quickly by anger and hurt over Jesus's nap. Fear has a way of turning us toward self-preservation, so in their fear, the disciples naturally became self-focused. They woke Jesus and accused Him of not caring about them.

3. Why is it ironic that the disciples asked Jesus, "Do you not care that we are perishing?"

4. Why is it so easy to lose sight of the truth when we're afraid?

5. Review 4:39. When Jesus woke from His nap, where did He point His rebuke?

    A. The wind and the sea

    B. The disciples for their fear and anger

    C. The devil

    D. The false god in control of weather

6. What does this reveal about the power of Jesus?

7. What does this reveal about the heart of Jesus?

8. If you were a disciple in that boat in the storm, how would that have made you feel?

Jesus didn't rebuke His disciples' fear. Instead, He rebuked the *source* of their fear. And with three words, a severe storm ended and an equally severe calm fell instantly. No residual waves or even a rocking boat—just stillness and peace.

9. **Using a Greek lexicon, look up the word *great* (used to describe the calm in 4:39) and write down what you find.**

Once the source of the disciples' fear was supernaturally handled, Jesus talked to them about something that was a bigger issue than a life-threatening storm—the issue of their hearts. The initial emotion of being afraid of something frightening is a natural part of life, but Jesus addressed their *response* to their emotions.

10. How do you typically respond when you feel fearful?

11. **Review 4:40.** What correlation did Jesus draw between fear and faith?

12. **Read Psalm 56:3.** What did David say about fear?

At the end of this story, the disciples were filled with great fear and questioning who Jesus was. This may seem to contradict the words He had *just* said to them about fear. But in the original language, the fear they experienced in the storm and the fear they experienced after watching Jesus calm it were two very different words.

13. **Read the definitions of *afraid* (4:40) and *fear* (4:41) below.** Why is it important to understand the difference between the two?

- Afraid (4:40): *deilos*—timid, cowardice, scared

- Fear (4:41): *phobeō*—struck with amazement, startled

There is a human fear that can cause us to run away from something, and there is a supernatural fear that invites us to fall on our face in worship and draw near to God. The disciples had just watched Jesus, being fully man and fully God, put an immediate and supernatural end to a life-threatening situation, and it left them in awe to be in the presence of the holy God-Man, who both served them *and* saved them.

14. **Read Luke 5:1–8.** What was Peter's response to God's holiness?

15. **Read Isaiah 6:1–5.** What was Isaiah's response to God's holiness?

In today's reading, we saw Jesus's humanity on display in His need to sleep. We also saw His deity on display in His authority over the natural world. Being fully God and fully man, Jesus is the only one who can provide a solution for the problem of sin that became abundantly clear to the disciples after the storm, to Peter after the catch, and to Isaiah after seeing the Lord in the temple.

16. When you reflect on God's holiness and your sin, which of the two types of fear do you feel? Why?

Mark 5:1–20

 **READ MARK 5:1–20**

Most people would rather be known by their giftings and accomplishments than by their weaknesses and low points. But in today's reading, a transformative encounter with Jesus left one man eager to share about his inability to fix his own problems.

Jesus and His disciples had barely stepped foot on dry ground when a man with an unclean spirit—a demonic spirit—aggressively ran toward them and fell at Jesus's feet. This was undoubtedly a jarring welcome to the Gentile region of the Gerasenes on the east side of the Sea of Galilee.

1. **Read Luke 8:27 and review Mark 5:3–6.** List all of your observations about the man with the unclean spirit.

Without stopping to address what kind of evil the man had done, whether he was at fault for his own demonic possession, or whether he'd ever tried to get better, Jesus saw a hurting person who was created in the image of God. Jesus didn't let the man's nakedness, aggression, or supernatural strength stop Him from seeing the man's humanity and restoring him.

2. When confronted with people who have obvious needs, are you more likely to react to their humanity or their appearance?

Even Jesus's own disciples didn't fully understand Him (as we saw in 4:41), but the many unclean spirits in the man bowing at His feet knew *exactly* who Jesus was. These demons even invoked God in an attempt to be spared. Though the demons believed in God and had all the correct information, they didn't surrender to Him or worship Him. This serves as an important reminder that having all the right information isn't the same thing as having a new heart. Information can't change hearts—only God can do that.

3. Look up 5:7 in a Bible commentary. Why did the demon say Jesus's name and full identity out loud?

This local superstition about having power over someone when using their name was a feeble attempt by the demons to gain the upper hand in an obviously uneven matchup.

When Jesus asked the unclean spirit his name in return, the demon gave the descriptive moniker "Legion." In Roman military terms, a legion was a unit of six thousand men, which indicated that the unclean spirit in this man was multiple demons. The moniker was like that of a biker who goes by the name Tank. It wasn't his name, but a description of who he was.

4. Consider the conversation between Jesus and the demons about the pigs. What does this reveal about Jesus's ability? What does this reveal about His heart?

5. Read John 10:10. How did the demons in the herd of pigs reflect Satan's goals?

6. Why is it important for us to understand the schemes of the enemy?

While we can be encouraged that Jesus's authority over the works of the enemy is absolute, passages like Ephesians 6:10–20 encourage believers to be on guard. Until Christ returns, our world is still corrupted by sin, and the enemy will pursue opportunities to steal, kill, and destroy.

7. Review 5:14–17. How did the locals respond? Is this surprising? Why or why not?

8. Do you see yourself in their responses at all?

The people of the Gerasenes seem to be more afraid of a free man in his right mind than a chaotic, demon-possessed man with supernatural strength! They were also far more concerned with what was lost in the herd of pigs than what was gained for the man who had been freed. They begged Jesus to leave their town, and He did.

9. Why do you think Jesus didn't let the formerly possessed man come with Him? What greater calling did Jesus give him instead?

When Jesus returned to the region of the Decapolis (Mark 7:31–37), an entire crowd showed up to see Him. Their interest was likely a direct result of this one man sharing the story of Jesus. When he was in the midst of his most hopeless situation, broken and tormented, he encountered the One who would set him free—not just temporarily, but for eternity.

10. What story of your own God-given freedom can you share with the people in your life?

Mark 5:21–43

 **READ MARK 5:21-43**

As a ruler in the synagogue, Jairus was likely a respected authority in his community. But he had no power to heal his dying daughter, so he begged Jesus to intervene. As they were on their way, a crowd impeded their progress. It's easy to imagine this would frustrate Jairus and that he may have felt even more desperate when Jesus stopped to ask who had touched Him. This was a strange question for two reasons: First, He was in a crowd, so there were many people touching Him. Second, the God who can read thoughts and minds certainly knew who had touched Him.

The woman who touched Him had been sick for as long as Jairus's daughter had been alive. Her need was immense, and her actions were risky, but Jesus paused to focus on her.

1. **Look up Mark 5:25 in a Bible commentary.** Why was this woman's disease more than just a physical problem?

Because she was legally unclean, it's possible she hadn't experienced human touch in twelve years. She had seen a litany of doctors, but medicine in the first century was rudimentary at best. Her pursuit of healing left her financially ruined as her pain mounted. She knew there was only one way she could be cured.

2. In our desperation, we've all looked somewhere other than Jesus for hope and healing. List a few things you've put your hope in that have led to more pain and/or bankruptcy (moral or financial).

There's a good chance she'd learned about Jesus from her primary community—other outcasts. Who was this man who served even those who had been shunned? Based on what she'd heard about Him (and possibly some local superstitions about articles of clothing holding special power) she was confident that merely touching the fringed tassels of His prayer shawl would heal her. So she broke the rules, wading into a throng of people, then touched His clothes in faith. She was instantly and miraculously healed.

3. Look up 5:30–34 in a commentary. This woman had attempted to fly under the radar for her healing. How did Jesus's question show kindness to her?

By asking the question in front of the crowd, Jesus was able to tell everyone not only that she had been healed but *why* she was healed. It wasn't a magic garment that healed her—it was the source of her faith, Jesus Himself.

Despite this powerful, generous healing, there was one person in this crowd who might not have been as moved by the scene.

4. What do you imagine Jairus was thinking and feeling when he found out his daughter had died during Jesus's conversation with the woman?

While we can't know for sure, Jesus's response gives us a glimpse into Jairus's thoughts. Jesus told Jairus not to fear but to believe. It's almost as if He was telling Jairus, "I know you had a plan, but even though you can't see it right now, My plan is better."

At Jairus's house, the local funeral customs were in full swing. Traditionally, even the poor hired at least two professional mourners when a spouse died to increase the public display of grief. But for a man of importance like Jairus, there were likely multiple mourners on hand. Their paid grief quickly turned to ridicule when Jesus insisted that the girl was simply asleep and not dead.

5. What do you think Jesus meant when He said she was asleep?

6. What does that reveal about the power of Jesus?

After kicking everyone out except for the girl's parents, Jesus said the same thing many parents around the region had likely said to their daughters early that morning—it's a tender phrase that loosely translates to "Sweetie, it's time to get up." And she did.

In some ways, these two stories of healing seem to be polar opposites: The woman was poor and nameless, while Jairus was respected and had means. The woman was unable to enter the community, while Jairus was a leader in the community.

7. What similarities do these two stories share?

The woman displayed the difference between simply bumping into Jesus and reaching for Him in faith. Jairus displayed that Jesus's plan and timing are always perfect. And for both of them, the physical touch of Jesus brought great joy—because He's where the joy is.

8. What stood out to you most in this week's study? Why?

9. What did you learn or relearn about God and His character this week?

DAY 6

Corresponding Psalm & Prayer

 **READ PSALM 29**

1. What correlation do you see between Psalm 29 and this week's study of Jesus and His kingdom?

2. What portions of this psalm stand out to you most?

3. Close by praying this prayer aloud:

Father,

I praise You for Your power over all Your creation. I praise You for Your holiness—for being set apart. Even in Your holiness, You still chose to enter into a relationship with fallen humanity. You are so merciful to us and don't show us the wrath we deserve. Through the work of Your Son, Jesus, You made a way for us to be part of Your eternal family! Thank You!

I confess that I've turned away from You at times. Some days, I've been like the rocky soil—I've doubted Your goodness when I faced trials. Other days, I've been like the thorny soil—my heart has been turned away by the flashy things of the world and You've taken a backseat. And sometimes my heart is just hard—I've refused to hear or acknowledge the truth. I repent of the times when I've leaned into those evil attitudes. Instead, I turn to You and ask You to soften the soil of my heart. Only You can do it.

Help me to hear and understand. Help me to see and perceive. Grant me steadfastness so that whether I encounter lack or abundance, my eyes will stay fixed on You, not on my circumstances or the world around me. And when I'm afraid, help me take my fear to the right place—to You—in the midst of the storm.

I surrender my life to You, Lord—every moment of my day, each decision I make, I yield my will and way to Your perfect will and way.

I love You too. Amen.

DAY 7

Rest, Catch Up, or Dig Deeper

 **WEEKLY CHALLENGE**

In Mark 4:40, Jesus juxtaposed fear with faith. We want to aim to grow in faith and to reduce the power fear has in our lives. This week, make space in your schedule to honestly contemplate at least one source of fear in your life. To help your heart trust in the Lord, write down at least one characteristic or attribute of God that displays His power over each source of fear you've listed. Then find a verse that points to that attribute of God and make note of it as well.

The human instinct to be afraid when something is scary or life-threatening—either real or perceived—is a natural response. Regardless of what your journey through fear and anxiety looks like, we can all benefit from regular reminders of who God is, which help us grow in our faith in Him even in the midst of our fears. He is the God who draws near to you when you struggle with fear.

Mark 6:

The Servant's Rejection and Response

Scripture to Memorize

And they came to Jericho. And as he was leaving Jericho with his disciples and a great crowd, Bartimaeus, a blind beggar, the son of Timaeus, was sitting by the roadside.

Mark 10:46

DAILY BIBLE READING

Day 1: Mark 6:1–6

Day 2: Mark 6:7–13

Day 3: Mark 6:14–29

Day 4: Mark 6:30–44

Day 5: Mark 6:45–56

Day 6: Psalm 73

Day 7: Catch-Up Day

Corresponds to Day 290 of *The Bible Recap*.

WEEKLY CHALLENGE

See page 120 for more information.

Mark 6:1–6

 **READ MARK 6:1-6**

After an eventful time in Capernaum, Jesus and His disciples headed to His hometown of Nazareth. It was roughly a twenty-five-mile walk—approximately a two-day journey—to this town of five hundred to a thousand people. But this relatively obscure place would soon be put on the map because of its connection to Jesus.

On the Sabbath, Jesus showed up to teach in the synagogue, and He would've had a captive audience.

1. **Review 6:2.** What was the people's initial emotional response?

Luke's account of this story fills in some of the details Mark skips over and helps us see this event with greater clarity.

2. **Read Luke 4:16–22.** How did the crowd respond to Jesus's declaration of being the Messiah?

3. Read Luke 4:23–29. What did Jesus say that turned them from astonishment to anger?

4. Why might that have been particularly offensive to this Jewish crowd?

Jesus mentioned two of Israel's great prophets working among Gentiles as a way of pointing to God's salvation extending beyond the Jews. It was unthinkable to them that God would welcome outsiders into His family—especially the Gentiles they'd spent their lives avoiding—and it infuriated them. But God's grace goes further than they ever could have imagined!

5. Is there anyone you find it hard to imagine God's grace extending to?

In a matter of minutes, Jesus's synagogue audience went from being astonished to offended. And Jesus was far from surprised at their response. The crowds who knew Jesus and His family rejected Him and His message.

6. Why do you think Jesus could do no mighty work in Nazareth? Read the parallel account of this verse in Matthew 13:58 to inform your answer.

Some say it's possible that the people's faith held the key to unlock His healing power, and since they had no faith, He had no power. But we've seen Jesus demonstrate His power even in spaces where people doubted Him. The more likely reality is that the people who needed healing simply did not come to Jesus at all. What a tragic loss. Jesus invites us to come to Him and ask of Him—He has power to do the mighty works we need and desire!

7. What needs and desires do you want to ask Jesus to respond to today?

Mark 6:7–13

 **READ MARK 6:7–13**

Remember when Jesus first chose His apostles? In today's reading those twelve men stepped into a new aspect of their calling.

1. Review 3:13–19 for a refresher on who these apostles are. According to this passage, what was Jesus's purpose for them?

Up to this point, the apostles had been in the "being with Him" phase of His plan. They had traveled with Jesus for roughly a year, learning from Him as part of His broader entourage of disciples. In today's reading, Jesus moved into the "send them out" phase. They were to act as His representatives and get hands-on experience in ministry. He gathered the twelve and shared His plan before He launched them out, giving them instructions and imparting the divine power necessary for the work He was calling them to accomplish.

2. **Review 6:7–11 alongside the list below.** Draw a line through false information and put a check next to accurate information about Jesus's preparation of His disciples.

☐ They were to stay in as many houses as possible on their journey.

☐ They were sent out in teams of two.

☐ He guaranteed they would be positively received.

☐ Shaking the dust off their feet was to be a sign of approval.

☐ He gave them the ability to control forces of nature.

☐ They were instructed to bring only a staff, sandals, and one tunic.

☐ He gave them power over demonic spirits.

The apostles wouldn't have had any qualms about being sent out in community and with Jesus's authority. But when Jesus got to the part about what they were supposed to bring with them, there might have been some raised eyebrows. Talk about traveling light! Jesus's packing list would have made even the most minimalist ancient Jew start to sweat. The apostles were to bring less than the bare minimum—no backup outfits, no food provisions, no storage, and no funds.

3. In addition to how to do ministry, what do you think Jesus wanted them to experience and learn?

By charging the apostles to take *less* with them, Jesus created an opportunity for them to trust God *more*. They were stripped of self-reliance. As they went about their journey, they would face the challenge of walking in faith and know the privilege of seeing how God would provide.

But even more than the limited packing list, they may have been taken aback to learn that they would face opposition to their ministry. When

Jesus directed them to shake the dust from their feet anywhere people refused to listen to their message, He was implying that they'd face rejection. Every experience the apostles had with Jesus was a part of their preparation. They'd watched Him seek and serve the least and the lost. They'd seen His power on display. They'd experienced the joy and gratitude of those who were healed. But they'd also seen Jesus be rejected, doubted, and accused.

It's fitting that the apostles were sent out on the heels of Jesus's less than positive reception in Nazareth. He modeled what it looks like to persevere in proclaiming the truth. Rejection didn't sway Jesus or slow Him down. He knew that even though many would doubt, many would believe. The apostles were called to follow His example and move forward with a clear conscience knowing they'd been faithful to His calling even when things didn't go as they'd hoped.

4. Review 6:12–13. After receiving Jesus's instructions, what did the apostles do?

5. What was their message to the people?

6. Read 1:4 and 1:14–15. Who else shared this message?

The apostles didn't just sit around after Jesus called them to go out. They went! They taught what He taught and did what He did. They preached the message of repentance, inviting people to turn away from sin and toward God. They brought healing and hope to many who were sick and broken along the way. Their obedience made an impact that mattered for the kingdom!

While we aren't members of the original twelve apostles, we're all sent in His authority into our various spheres of influence to carry good news and do good works as representatives of His kingdom. The reality of rejection and opposition is just as real as it was for the apostles, but so is the opportunity to be a part of God's eternal, transformative work in the lives of others.

7. Has fear of the unknown or fear of how you might be received kept you from stepping out in faith to share the gospel or minister with others? If so, describe how this has impacted you.

Just as He did with the apostles, God can equip you with all you need to spread the good news of Jesus—even if you feel you have very little of what you may need, and even when you face opposition. Ask Him to increase your confidence *in Him* in the face of those fears. Ask Him to continue to teach you how to be His faithful ambassador wherever you go!

Mark 6:14–29

Mark breaks up the account of the apostles' travels with an update on JTB, who was arrested in 1:14. In today's reading, we get the details surrounding his imprisonment and learn that this faithful forerunner of Jesus ended his ministry as a martyr at the hands of Herod.

Herod Antipas—the "King" Herod in our reading—wasn't really a king. He was a ruler in the Roman empire during Jesus's ministry, but his actual title was tetrarch. The first time we encounter him in Mark is in connection with JTB's execution, and the next time we'll hear of him will be for his involvement in Jesus's crucifixion.

1. **Do a web search for Herod Antipas and his family to help you answer the following questions.**

> Who was he a successor of?

> How was that individual relevant in the timeline of Jesus's life? (Hint: See Matthew 2:1–18.)

> As a tetrarch, how much of the political division of Judah was Herod Antipas placed over?

What region did Herod Antipas rule over?

As Jesus grew in popularity, so did murmurings about His identity. The crowds were generally confused about who He was. His ministry connected in uncanny ways with prophecy about Elijah and reminded people of the prophets of old. Talk about Jesus and His miraculous power had made its way to Herod, who was convinced that Jesus was somehow a reincarnation of JTB, the man he'd had killed.

2. **Use the Venn diagram below to compare and contrast the lives and ministries of Jesus and JTB.** Based on what we know of Herod's experience with JTB, what similarities do you think would've led to Herod's confusion about Jesus's identity?

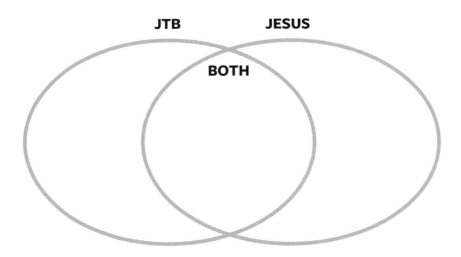

Like Jesus, JTB had unwaveringly preached a message about repentance and forgiveness of sins, and that would've struck many and stuck with Herod. He wouldn't have had many other encounters with this kind of teaching, so when he heard about Jesus, a prophet preaching in a new way about the kingdom of God, it would've been easy to associate Him with JTB. It's also possible Herod's guilty conscience over JTB's death contributed to his confusion about Jesus's identity.

3. **Review 6:17–20 and match the people to the descriptions that fit.**

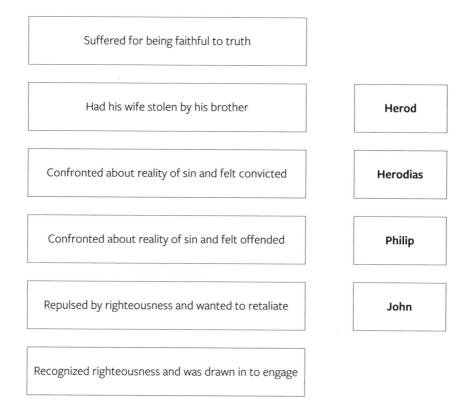

Suffered for being faithful to truth	
Had his wife stolen by his brother	**Herod**
Confronted about reality of sin and felt convicted	**Herodias**
Confronted about reality of sin and felt offended	**Philip**
Repulsed by righteousness and wanted to retaliate	**John**
Recognized righteousness and was drawn in to engage	

JTB was thrown in prison after he boldly called out the sin of a power-hungry couple, Herod and Herodias. Their marriage was both incestuous and adulterous, but JTB didn't run away from the rebuke of rich royals. Herodias was especially displeased. Given JTB's influence, his truth telling was a threat to her and her husband's reputation and power.

Roughly two years later, JTB was still imprisoned, Herodias was still holding a grudge, and Herod was throwing himself a birthday bash. Men of status and influence from across Galilee attended this celebration, and Herod likely spared no expense for it. As part of the entertainment, Herodias's daughter performed a dance for the crowd that was probably far from G-rated. The customary style of dance in these settings was more of a striptease than a tap recital. Herod was pleased by his niece-turned-stepdaughter's production and, in an attempt to wow his guests and win their approval, he made the girl an over-the-top promise he would soon regret.

4. In your own words, describe what happened in 6:23–29.

Herod's vow to give up to half of his kingdom wasn't literal. It was an idiom of the day that his daughter, wife, and guests would've understood to mean that he was willing to give a gift of incredible value. Herodias seized the opportunity to use her husband's foolishness to satisfy her desire for vengeance, taking advantage of her daughter as a pawn in the plot. And Herodias got what she wanted: a public and extravagant execution of JTB. The forerunner of Jesus died by beheading, and his head was handed to Herodias on a platter.

5. What does Herodias's willingness to choose JTB's beheading over extravagant material gifts reveal about her heart?

In this account we see the three main characters—JTB, Herodias, and Herod Antipas—being motivated by what mattered to them the most. Herodias was so controlled by her sin that she was willing to put to death the one who pointed it out. Herod was so concerned about his reputation and consumed by his fear of man that he shrunk back from opportunity after opportunity to do what was right. And JTB was so committed to living for the kingdom of God and the truth that he was willing to die for it.

JTB's motivation in confronting the evil that he saw in the lives of Herod and his wife would've been to call them to repentance, not just to call them out. He told them things that were hard to hear, but for the sake of their hearts. Herodias and Herod had sinned greatly, but they weren't outside the reach of God's grace.

The message JTB died in his commitment to proclaim is the message that Jesus would die in His commitment to fulfill. Because of Jesus's finished work on the cross, we can let go of the sin that controls us and grab hold of the forgiveness He made available to us!

Mark 6:30–44

 **READ MARK 6:30–44**

When the twelve disciples ("learners, followers") Jesus sent out as apostles ("messengers") returned, they told Him about all they'd said and done on their mission. The crowds surrounded them while they talked, and there was so much happening that they couldn't even find time for a meal. In the midst of this chaos, Jesus gave them their next assignment.

1. **Review 6:31.** Break down Jesus's instruction into each of the following categories.

Who?

What?

When?

Where?

Why?

How?

2. What do the context and specifics of Jesus's command reveal about what He views as important?

Jesus could've told the disciples to do a number of things, in a number of places, for a number of reasons—but the first thing He called them to after they came back from ministering to people was rest. In His humanity, Jesus understood the toll that pouring themselves out in the service of others would have on their minds, bodies, and spirits. He had led them into the important work they'd completed, and here He was leading them to the equally important rest they needed.

While Jesus and the disciples were on a boat en route to rest, word got out about where they were headed. By the time they landed on the shore, their desolate place was filled with more desperate people who had run from all over the region for the chance to be in Jesus's presence. This was no small crowd. This was thousands of needy people following Jesus and begging for His help. And despite His desire to get away, He had compassion on them.

3. Sometimes we miss out on the richness of words we're familiar with because we assume we already know what they mean. Let's dive into the word *compassion*. First, write your own definition of compassion.

4. **Now look up** *compassion* **in a dictionary.**

5. **Finally, use a Greek lexicon to find the specific word used for Jesus's compassion in 6:34.** Summarize what it means.

Splagchnizomai, the Greek word for compassion used here, shows up twelve times in the New Testament, and it's only used to reference Jesus or someone in a parable who points us to Him. Jesus literally felt for the crowds. He looked out at the masses and saw shepherdless sheep—they were like vulnerable starving animals unable to feed themselves, defenseless against danger.

6. The imagery of sheep and shepherds shows up throughout the Old Testament in reference to Israel and its spiritual leaders. **Read the following Old Testament passages.** Underneath each one, write what you notice about the situations of the sheep and the identity of the shepherds.

Ezekiel 34:1–10

Ezekiel 34:23–24

Zechariah 10:1–3

Isaiah 40:10–11

Micah 5:2–4

7. Do you notice any significant themes?

Jesus stepped into the situation with the heart of the Good Shepherd. He sensed the needs of the people and did the most compassionate thing He could to serve them. He taught them.

8. How is sharing God's Word one of the most loving acts of service we can offer?

9. How does it benefit and bless believers and nonbelievers alike?

Jesus could've gone out to meet the crowds shouting, "Who needs healing, money, or a miracle?" and there would've been thousands of people jumping up and down with hands raised. But Jesus knew that, more than anything, they needed to understand who He was and what He came to accomplish.

Jesus prioritized the spiritual, but He didn't ignore the physical, emotional, or material. We saw this play out as it got late and the disciples pointed out that people's stomachs were starting to rumble. For reference, there were 5,000 men *and their families* in the crowd—roughly 15,000 mouths to feed. The disciples suggested that Jesus send the crowds away to find food, but Jesus's solution was for the disciples to give them something to eat.

10. Jesus and the disciples had different vantage points on the same situation. What was informing each party's perspective? What obstacles or opportunities might they have had in mind?

Disciples	Jesus
Vantage point:	Vantage point:
Obstacles/opportunities:	Obstacles/opportunities:

At Jesus's direction, the disciples took inventory of what they had on hand and came back with a report of a meager five loaves and two fish. Unfazed, Jesus organized the crowds, blessed the meal, broke the loaves, and gave the food to the disciples to distribute to the people. As they went from group to group, the disciples were never in short supply. Every single person ate and was satisfied.

A reality the disciples couldn't fathom moments earlier had just happened. Jesus had supplied everything they needed to carry out what He had called them to. And each of the twelve men had a basketful of leftovers as a tangible reminder that Jesus had authority over nature—*and* that He cared.

Apart from Jesus, the apostles wouldn't have been able to serve the crowds spiritually or physically. They didn't have the eyes to perceive needs or the power to provide for needs like Jesus did. But because they were *with* Him, they were part of something amazing! Even in our limitations, God invites us into His mission. He loves to use ordinary people. When we willingly offer ourselves to be used for His glory and the good of others, He can do more than we can imagine in and through us.

11. When you think about your resources (time, energy, money, giftings, abilities, etc.), where are you tempted to feel lack, which leads you away from trusting God or serving others?

End today by writing out a short prayer thanking God for what He has given you, even where it feels like little. Ask Him to remind you of who He is and show you how He can work in the midst of your perceived weakness, deficiency, or need so that He would glorify Himself and bless others.

Mark 6:45–56

READ MARK 6:45–56

The primary focus of Jesus's ministry was getting people to grasp eternal spiritual realities, but among His steady stream of faithful followers and seekers, most people were stuck in temporal patterns of thinking.

It had been a long day of ministering to the multitudes near Capernaum, and things were winding down on the Jewish (western) side of the Sea of Galilee. Jesus told the disciples to go ahead of Him to Bethsaida, on the eastern side, while He sent the crowds home.

1. Referencing the map below, note the proximity of Capernaum and Bethsaida.

After everyone was gone, Jesus headed up a mountain to pray. We saw Jesus pull away for prayer in Mark 1, and we'll continue to see this rhythm in His life. Before big decisions, during intense moments, and even after the exhilarating chaos that surrounded His miracles in today's reading, Jesus prized spending time with God the Father and intentionally sought out time to be alone with Him.

2. When it comes to spending restful or prayerful time with God, what are your regular rhythms?

3. Write down at least one thing you might gain from restful or prayerful time with God that varies from what you might gain through Bible study and service.

4. What is one practical way you can take a step toward prioritizing restful or prayerful time with Him this week?

While Jesus was resting in His Father's presence, the disciples were struggling out at sea. A harsh, heavy wind fought against them, and regardless of how hard they were *row, row, rowing*, they weren't *go, go, going*. They had listened to Jesus's instruction when He told them to go across to the other side, but now they were in a tough situation, and He was nowhere to be found.

5. Obedience to God doesn't always mean smooth sailing in the circumstance of our lives. What promises from Scripture can you cling to in difficult situations when you can't understand what God is doing? (Use a Bible study tool or do a web search if you need help.)

Jesus wasn't physically with the disciples, but He hadn't forgotten, failed, or abandoned them. He saw them on the troubled waters and set out on foot to meet them.

When reading the Bible, knowing how time was kept isn't essential, but it can be helpful for context. Research Roman night watches using a Bible study resource, and estimate the time frame of events specified in this account.*

6. What time or time frame is referenced in 6:47? What time does it equate to in our modern time system?

*Carolyn Hurst has a helpful graphic at https://www.passiontoknowmore.com/post/2016 -1-19-what-hour-is-that.

7. What time or time frame is referenced in 6:48? What time does it equate to in our modern time system?

8. What does this add to your understanding?

Jesus walked calmly across the waves He would soon still. But as the disciples caught a glimpse of a figure approaching their boat, they were filled with fear. Jewish tradition taught that demons wandered around in the wilderness and at sea, so they probably thought an evil spirit was coming toward them. Jesus immediately called out to the tired and frightened crew. "Take heart; it is I. Do not be afraid."

9. Jesus gave His disciples two imperatives. "Do not be afraid" is pretty straightforward, but what does it mean to "take heart"?

10. Why is Jesus's identity central to the comfort and encouragement He was calling the disciples into?

Imagine being trapped in a blazing fire in your apartment building, desperate for help, and your one-hundred-year-old neighbor Miss Eunice shows up and says, "Cheer up, honey! I'm here. Don't you worry, now." Miss Eunice may be present and optimistic, but frankly, she's in just as much trouble as you are.

Jesus's words weren't deluded positivity—they were an assurance to His disciples that His presence and power would change their circumstances. He stepped into their boat and the winds completely stopped. Surprisingly, they were surprised. They had just seen Jesus display this same Divine authority over nature in feeding the crowds, but their hearts were too hard for the truth to fully sink in.

11. Briefly describe a significant time when God met you in your circumstances with His peace, power, or provision.

12. How do your experience and knowledge of His Word challenge you in any areas of unbelief?

When the boat hit land, Jesus and the disciples were greeted by a clamoring crowd that was hungry for healing. Many came from near and far carrying people on beds and laying them at Jesus's feet, desperate for Him to bring relief from their sickness and disease.

13. The people recognized Jesus and were eager to be in His presence, but in what way might they have missed who He was?

Jesus showed mercy and worked miracles, but they were never meant to be the point. The people in the crowd may have received healing in their bodies through touching Him, but the true healing He came into the world to bring could only come through His teaching.

It's easy to seek God for what He can do for us, but our greatest need is always a deeper understanding of who He is. When God changes hard life circumstances, it's a blessing; but the generous gift of repentance and faith is the best thing we could ever experience, because it puts us into a right relationship with Him, and He's where the joy is!

14. What stood out to you most in this week's study? Why?

15. What did you learn or relearn about God and His character this week?

Corresponding
Psalm & Prayer

 **READ PSALM 73**

1. What correlation do you see between Psalm 73 and this week's study of Jesus and His kingdom?

2. What portions of this psalm stand out to you most?

3. Close by praying this prayer aloud:

Father,

   You are so good! I praise You for Your compassionate heart. You have blessed all creation, and I'm grateful to be not only Your creation but also Your child, thanks to the finished work of Your Son, Jesus.

I confess that I've ignored Your goodness and compassion. I've envied the wicked at times—their ease of life or the abundance they've gained through evil. I've treated prosperity as a marker of Your goodness, and I've grown angry or frustrated with You when I haven't received the things I thought my obedience had earned me. And because of my self-righteous attitude, I've sometimes found it hard to extend grace to others. I repent of not loving others well. I repent of treating obedience like a token I can exchange for the life I expected.

Thank You for granting me eyes to see the truth: Your holiness and goodness, Your wisdom and beauty. Help me to treasure You above all else. Help me to grasp the eternal realities that Jesus pointed to so often. Keep me near to You and make me attentive to You throughout my days. Like the disciples, help me to go where You send me and do what You've called me to do. Grow my compassion for those I encounter so that I'll look more like Your Son, Jesus, and serve them like He did. You are the author and perfecter of my faith, so give me the faith I'll need for every step of that process.

I surrender my life to You, Lord—every moment of my day, each decision I make, I yield my will and way to Your perfect will and way.

I love You too. Amen.

Rest, Catch Up, or Dig Deeper

WEEKLY CHALLENGE

The story of Herod and JTB reveals how God often lovingly serves us by using others to speak words of correction in our lives. The Holy Spirit can use the words of others to bring us to conviction and repentance. Those two things are gifts that help us follow God more closely and experience Him more fully. However, our pride can get in the way of receiving even true things brought to our attention by trusted people. To deal a blow to our pride, we can lean in and listen with humility to learn what God might want to teach us. We can practice receiving the gifts of conviction and repentance with gratitude, opening ourselves up to correction and growth!

This week, reach out to another Christ-follower you respect and trust who knows you well. Ask them to think through what they know of you and to prayerfully consider if they see any red flags (blatant sin) or yellow flags (worrisome traits) in your life. Ask them to share those with you at some point later in the week. Prayerfully process what they say and ask God to help you rightly respond. (*A word of caution: The person you ask may not accurately perceive your actions or your motives, so this is not a call to receive their words as truth—this is a call to lean into growth and humility by seeking out correction from others.*)

Mark 7–8:

The Law of the Servant

DAILY BIBLE READING

Day 1: Mark 7:1–23

Day 2: Mark 7:24–37

Day 3: Mark 8:1–10

Day 4: Mark 8:11–26

Day 5: Mark 8:27–38

Day 6: Psalm 51

Day 7: Catch-Up Day

Corresponds to Days 292–293 of *The Bible Recap*.

WEEKLY CHALLENGE

See page 144 for more information.

Mark 7:1–23

 **READ MARK 7:1–23**

In today's reading, Jesus was approached by Pharisees and scribes. They traveled from Jerusalem to Galilee—roughly 80 miles—to accuse Jesus and His disciples of breaking a law. That's a trip of eight to ten days just to rebuke a rural rabbi and His small crew of followers.

The Pharisees prided themselves on upholding what God commanded, but they added myriad extra rules of their own that made life unnecessarily harder for everyone. They took the commandments and laws in Scripture and "built a fence" around those laws to make sure no one got anywhere close to breaking them. This fence was what Jesus referred to as "traditions." For example, if God's law said the speed limit was 65 miles per hour, they'd build their fence at 55 miles per hour and ticket people for driving 60. And in this analogy, Jesus would often intentionally drive at 60 miles per hour and point out that He wasn't breaking *God's law*—He was breaking *their tradition*. To put it plainly, laws were made by God and traditions were made by men.

1. **Review 7:1–13.** How many times does Jesus use the word *tradition*?

The only thing these guys loved more than making rules was enforcing them. What started out as a good endeavor—not wanting to break God's law—turned into legalism, pride, and oppression. According to the Pharisees, Jews were expected to wash not only their hands but also their cups, pots, bowls, and so on. When they approached Jesus, He was eating with His disciples and some of them hadn't washed their hands before the meal.

2. **Read Exodus 30:17–21.** What are the requirements for washing hands from God's commandments?

The Pharisees thought if priests should wash their hands and feet before entering the tabernacle, then all Jews should wash their hands before they ate anything, just in case. But that was not God's law; that was just how they *enforced* God's law. In 7:8, Jesus rebuked them and said, "You leave the commandment of God and hold to the tradition of men." Jesus knew the Pharisees were more concerned with *looking* holy than with what it meant to *be* holy. They even went so far as to cancel out some of God's laws with new rules of their own that were more convenient to them. It allowed them to maintain a good reputation while still doing whatever they wanted.

3. What is a modern example of a tradition or rule competing with a law?

4. What traditions or rules have you created in your own Christian walk that aren't found in Scripture?

After Jesus rebuked the Pharisees about their pre-dinner rituals, He delivered a rebuke about the food itself. Not only would their dirty hands *not* defile them, but neither would the food they ate. In Jewish law, there were several foods that made a person "unclean," but Jesus—knowing He had come to fulfill all the purification laws—said there was nothing you could eat that could defile you. This would've been shocking to His hearers who had worked so hard to keep the food laws! He said things that go into their mouths aren't defiling, but the things that come out of their mouths are—their words reveal their hearts, and God is always after a heart-level purity.

5. **Read Jeremiah 17:9–10 and Matthew 12:33–34.** What do these passages say about our hearts?

6. **Review the list of thoughts and actions in 7:21–22.** List the three thoughts or actions you find yourself struggling with most.

7. Describe one example of how you've seen one of those thoughts or actions show up in your life this week.

8. **Use a Bible study tool to look up each thought or action you listed above.** Write out a verse that can help encourage and strengthen you as you face each of those three struggles.

It's easy to get lost in the do's and don'ts that we believe God wants us to observe. The good news is that it's not up to us to change our hearts. Ephesians 2:8–9 says we have been saved by grace, not as a result of our own doing. We are saved into a relationship with God because of His grace—unmerited favor—toward us through the finished work of Christ. With Jesus, it no longer matters if you eat the right foods, wash your hands the right way, or look like the "perfect" Christ-follower. Jesus knew we could never keep the law perfectly, so He came to live the perfect law on our behalf and fulfill it for us. We are set free from the law when we come into a relationship with Jesus. When we see Him clearly, we get to live from a foundation of love, not rules!

Mark 7:24–37

 **READ MARK 7:24–37**

In today's reading, Jesus left the Galilee region and headed north to Tyre and Sidon, a predominantly Gentile region. While Jews typically avoided going to Gentile areas, Jesus made it a point to not only go, but engage with a Syrophoenician (Gentile) woman who stopped Him to ask for help. She told Him about her demon-possessed daughter and begged Him to heal her.

1. **Read Matthew 15:21–28.** In Matthew's account of this story, how did the disciples respond to the woman?

Have you ever felt annoyed by someone who was asking for help? Have you ever preferred to avoid or ignore them? That's how the disciples felt. God had originally called the Jewish people to be set apart from the Gentiles—not because they were better than them, but because the Gentiles all worshiped other gods and the Jews were often tempted to intermarry with them and take on their false gods. But over time, this holiness technique morphed into a view of Gentiles as second-class citizens, commonly referred to as dogs.

At first glance, Jesus's response to the woman's plea could seem cruel, but He created a metaphor describing the priorities of His ministry and used it as a teaching moment for His disciples. When Jesus mentioned throwing the children's bread to dogs, He didn't use the standard derogatory term. Instead, He used an affectionate version of the word—the word often used of a beloved pet, not a stray nuisance. His words built a bridge—they were a subtle way of communicating a different type of relationship from what Jews typically had with Gentiles. And Jesus leaned in even more, taking steps across that bridge.

Even though she was a Gentile, Jesus chose to stop for her, against the disciples' wishes. He engaged her in conversation, even as He acknowledged that His main mission was for the people of Israel. Jesus often tested people through challenges like this to help them demonstrate their intentions. And the woman did not waver. She showed that she not only understood what Jesus was saying, but had the conviction and the faith to ask for His help anyway. It would've been easy for her to see His response as a no, but she was persistent. Jesus acknowledged and rewarded her faith, healing her daughter instantly.

2. Do you confidently approach God with your requests? Why or why not?

3. How does this challenge your own faith?

Jesus headed back home after His interaction with this Syrophoenician woman. There's no record of Him talking to anyone else while He was there. It's possible He and His followers made this four-day round trip just for her and her daughter.

When they returned to Galilee, Jesus was approached by a group begging Him to heal a man who was deaf and couldn't speak well. Jesus pulled the man aside, put His fingers in his ears, and touched his tongue, commanding his ears and mouth to "be opened." This is the only time Jesus healed someone in this way, and it's the only time the word *ephphatha* appears in the Bible. There was no script for how Jesus healed people—His miracles follow no pattern.

4. **Look up the following passages and match them to Jesus's method of healing.**

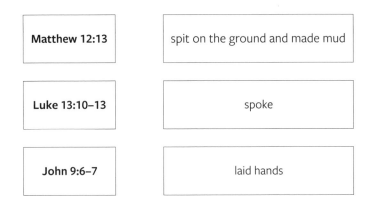

Matthew 12:13	spit on the ground and made mud
Luke 13:10–13	spoke
John 9:6–7	laid hands

The different ways Jesus chose to heal show that His power is not reliant on any special words or routine. No one could recreate it by copying Him. Being fully God, only He has ultimate authority to heal and change lives.

After the man was healed, Jesus asked the group not to tell anyone. However, they couldn't contain their excitement—they immediately spread the word about Jesus and His astonishing ways. Because of the way Jesus served him, the man who had a speech impediment used his newfound voice to become an evangelist!

5. When was the last time you were so excited about your faith that you couldn't help but share?

If nothing specific came to mind, ask God to provide you with that opportunity this week!

Mark 8:1–10

 **READ MARK 8:1–10**

Today's reading doesn't immediately make it clear, but Jesus and His disciples were in a Gentile region again. The crowd had been following Him for three days, and they had run out of food. Some of the people would've had a long walk home, and of course, this was a time when there were no restaurants or late-night markets, no gas stations or drive-throughs where they could grab a quick snack. If they had nothing with them, they likely wouldn't eat until they got home, which might have been a few days.

Jesus had compassion on them and chose to provide rather than just send them on their way. The disciples were skeptical that they could feed such a large crowd even though they had helped Him feed the five thousand not long ago. The disciples were first-hand witnesses to miracles, yet they still had to be reminded of Jesus's power in their lives *often*. They were quick to forget all the ways they saw Him working.

1. When—or in what areas of your life—do you tend to doubt God can provide for you?

2. How have you seen God provide in the past? Describe at least one instance. How can that give you confidence in your current circumstances?

Jesus gathered food from the disciples' own personal supply and found seven loaves and a few small dried fish. In Jesus's day, loaves were the size of a small cake, barely enough for a singular meal. He was starting off with not even enough to feed Him and His disciples, much less a crowd of four thousand. He gave thanks to God for the loaves and blessed the fish before He distributed both to the crowd. They had more than enough for everyone, and even gathered seven baskets full of leftovers. Jesus provided everything they needed and more!

3. The number seven shows up twice in this story: seven loaves and seven baskets of leftovers. Using a Bible study tool for research, describe what the number seven represented in ancient Judaism.

It's not a mistake that Jesus used the disciples' bread to provide for the massive Gentile crowd. Jesus was consistently showing them, through His ministry, that He was on mission for the Jews first, but also to include Gentiles in His kingdom—and the disciples would play a huge role in that eventually. There is not only *room* for both in the kingdom, but a *plan* for both to be included. Jesus came to save all who would repent of their sins, believe in His sufficiency, and follow Him.

4. This account of feeding the four thousand is similar to the feeding of the five thousand in 6:30–43, but they're unique in important ways. Fill in the table below.

	Mark 6:30–43	Mark 8:1–10
How many people did Jesus feed?		
Who was the crowd mostly made up of?		
Where did Jesus get the food to feed the crowd?		
How many loaves did they have?		
How many fish did they have?		
How many baskets were left over?		
What do these numbers represent?		

Jesus was purposeful in His ministry and miracles. In ancient Judaism, numbers had meaning and significance. In His first multiplication of food, Jesus fed the group primarily made up of Jews, using five loaves and two fish—seven total items. They had twelve baskets of leftovers, likely representing both the disciples and the tribes of Israel. In His second multiplication of food, Jesus showed the completion and perfection of His ministry by feeding the Gentiles. He used seven loaves and a "few" fish and gathered seven baskets of leftovers. Jesus was intentional in His timing, His process, and even symbolic details. He's attentive to it all!

5. What recent circumstance in your life could benefit from this reminder of what Jesus is attentive to and capable of? Write out a prayer asking God to increase your faith and display His power.

When performing these miracles, Jesus could've just stopped the multiplication when everyone was satisfied, or once they'd eaten enough to sustain themselves. But through these two stories, we see that He's able to provide *more* than we could possibly need. And at the heart of it all, Jesus *Himself* is what we truly need. And unlike bread or fish, He's where we find the only kind of abundance that won't fade or disappear.

Mark 8:11–26

 **READ MARK 8:11-26**

Today opens in Dalmanutha, a town not too far from Jesus's home base of Capernaum. The Pharisees approached Jesus there and demanded a sign from heaven. They'd witnessed many of Jesus's miracles but still wanted more. They argued with Him, trying to test Him, revealing that they weren't sincerely looking for a sign. Jesus was a direct threat to their power, so in asking for more signs, they were aiming to disprove who He said He was.

1. Have you ever been asked a question by someone who was only trying to prove their own point and wasn't interested in your answer? How did that feel?

Jesus sighed deeply. Knowing their questions came from hardened hearts, He refused to perform for them. Afterward, He and the disciples left in a boat but soon realized they were down to one loaf of bread. Given the bread-related miracles Jesus had done in front of them—twice—bread was the *last* thing these guys should've been concerned about. Jesus used the topic to warn them about the subtle yet pervasive attitude of the Pharisees and Herod. He referred to them as leaven that should be avoided. A quick note on leaven in case you don't bake often: It makes bread rise, and a small amount is all you need for an entire loaf. The Pharisees were self-centered, self-righteous, and self-reliant—all of which are postures that if given an inch, will take a mile. Their attitudes polluted all their so-called "good actions," corrupting everything they did.

2. Have you ever seen one bad attitude infiltrate a group or ruin an experience? Briefly describe what happened.

Instead of picking up on what Jesus was really saying, the disciples thought He was talking about the lack of bread again. Per usual, the disciples didn't understand the spiritual truths Jesus was preaching, despite how willing they were. But because they were genuinely seeking to understand—unlike the Pharisees, who were seeking to disprove—Jesus didn't rebuke them. Instead, He reminded them of all the ways they'd seen His power on display. He'd *just* finished feeding a crowd of four thousand, and before that, five thousand. He reminded them not only of how He provided for all those people, but of the amounts they had left over. He had shown them over and over that He was the Messiah they'd been waiting for, but they were slow to grasp this truth. Despite all He had done, His disciples didn't yet see with perfect clarity.

3. In what areas of your life have you found it hard to believe that Jesus is who He says He is?

Once the boat arrived in Bethsaida, Jesus was met by a group of people who'd brought a blind man to Him for healing. Instead of healing the man in front of everyone, Jesus took his hand and led him out of the village. Jesus used His saliva and laid hands on the man to grant him sight. But the man wasn't immediately healed. It's noteworthy that Mark chose to include this story, because so many of Mark's narratives include the word *immediately*.

4. **Using your favorite Bible study tool, do some research on why Jesus made this particular healing a two-step process.** Note what you find.

5. What other group of people did this two-step healing process point to?

We know that Jesus had the power to heal immediately—He's made that obvious. His insistence on healing the man's sight first partially, then fully, served as an illustration of how the disciples were gradually seeing His true identity as well. They had seen His miracles, which pointed to His divinity, but they didn't fully grasp that He was the Messiah. Soon, they would see it clearly.

After healing the man, Jesus urged him to not even go back into the village. Given that this was a Gentile region, Jesus was still operating with the messianic secret in mind, keeping His identity as the Messiah concealed among the Gentiles until the right time.

Jesus could have done the big showy signs the Pharisees demanded. He could have performed every miracle in the town square, shouted from the rooftops to make people watch, or pursued quick notoriety and fame. But He didn't. He was not the conquering king the Jews were expecting;

He was a humble servant to those who truly sought Him. He purposely brought Himself low, and He does the same for us today.

6. What does this tell you about the heart of God? Describe below, then say a prayer thanking Him for His heart toward His people.

DAY 5

Mark 8:27–38

READ MARK 8:27-38

In the center of Mark's gospel we encounter the turning point in Jesus's ministry. For this important scene, Jesus took His disciples on a sixty-mile round trip to Caesarea Philippi. In His day, this was the site of pagan ritual worship beyond our modern comprehension. Their acts of pagan worship consisted of human sacrifice—particularly of babies—and bestiality. If Jews were used to avoiding most Gentile areas, this particular spot was so drenched in wickedness that it would've set off all their internal alarms. Yet this was Jesus's destination of choice.

Imagine the disciples—likely filled with a mix of curiosity and fear—traveling to this site with their leader, who was taking them there intentionally. On this trip, He asked the disciples two questions: "Who do people say that I am?" followed by "Who do *you* say that I am?" He asked them those questions for their benefit, not His own. He didn't need an ego boost or a pep talk, and He wasn't looking for validation. Jesus knew how important it would be for them to be certain that He was the Son of God. Otherwise it would be easy to walk away or despair when trouble arose. Peter boldly answered correctly, acknowledging that Jesus was exactly who He'd said He was the entire time—the Christ! With this answer clarified and embedded in the disciples' hearts, Jesus revealed why it was important that they clung to that truth.

1. **Review 8:31.** In your own words, summarize what Jesus said was going to happen.

Jesus told them in blatant terms that He was going to be killed but then raised from the dead. Peter had the audacity to rebuke the one he'd just identified as the Christ, Son of the living God. It wasn't that Peter no longer believed Him, but a Messiah that would be persecuted and sacrificed was not part of Peter's plan. In Peter's eyes, the Messiah was supposed to overthrow Rome, not die a sinner's death.

2. **Using your favorite Bible study tool, do some research on what Jesus may have meant by His response to Peter's rebuke.**

"Get behind me, Satan" is an intense response! The disciples had gotten it wrong plenty of times before, but Jesus had never compared them to Satan or said Satan was at work in them, so this was a unique scenario, indeed. Some theologians say the cross was the worst thing that could happen to Satan—it sealed his fate and ultimate defeat, so he, more than anyone else, wanted to stop it from happening at any cost. He had attempted to thwart God's plan for redemption when he tempted Jesus in the wilderness. Some say Jesus was using a metaphor when He said, "Get behind me, Satan," and others say He was actually calling out Satan at work in Peter.

3. Which of these views do you hold or prefer and why?

In Mark's gospel, Jesus went on to predict His own death two more times after this, using the same pattern each time. When Jesus announced His death, the disciples responded—usually with a wrong answer—then Jesus gave a teaching on discipleship. There was a theme to His process: Recognition of the death and resurrection of Jesus always requires a response.

4. Review 8:34. List the three things Jesus called His disciples to do in response to the cross.

1.

2.

3.

Being a disciple ("learner, follower") doesn't come naturally—it requires that we deny ourselves, which is something none of us inherently want to do. We must repent and turn from our former lives of sin, but it doesn't stop at just a pivot. Next, we must take up our cross. The cross, in today's world, is a symbol of forgiveness, grace, hope, and love. But in Jesus's day, the only time a person carried a cross was on the way to their own death. So by saying "take up your cross," He wasn't asking His followers to carry some burden in their lives—such as a challenging relationship, a serious illness, or a disability. Carrying your cross is symbolic for following Jesus, no matter what it costs you and despite whatever may come. Lastly, He calls us to follow Him. Following Jesus is a full transformation from the inside out. When we enter into a relationship with Him, we get the presence of the Holy Spirit in our lives, and He empowers us to walk in step with Him.

5. Have you truly chosen to deny yourself, take up your cross, and follow Jesus?

6. If not, what is keeping you from trusting Him?

7. If yes, write a short prayer thanking God for revealing Himself to you.

As we reach this turning point in the gospel of Mark, we'll begin to see Jesus moving toward His death at a faster pace. He wouldn't be keeping the messianic secret among the Jews anymore, because His time had come. The revealing of His identity had begun, and it would soon be fulfilled in front of a crowd of followers, enemies, and skeptics. Even today, as He continues to reveal Himself to people, those who truly see Him move into spaces of greater freedom and joy, because He's where the joy is!

8. What stood out to you most in this week's study? Why?

9. What did you learn or relearn about God and His character this week?

Corresponding Psalm & Prayer

 **READ PSALM 51**

1. What correlation do you see between Psalm 51 and this week's study of Jesus and His kingdom?

2. What portions of this psalm stand out to you most?

3. Close by praying this prayer aloud:

Father,
    You are a God of steadfast love. You are a God of abundant mercy. You forgive the sins of Your children and You make us clean—what a gift! I praise You for Your goodness and mercy to me.

Father, I'm a sinner, and You are a safe place to acknowledge my sins, because You already know them all and Your Son, Jesus, has already paid for them all on the cross. So I confess my sins to You and ask You to make my heart clean. I repent of acting like a Pharisee at times—treating my own customs and preferences and traditions as though they are Your law. I repent of not wanting to help certain people. I turn away from my sinful thoughts and actions, and I turn to You, the source of my forgiveness and my hope for change.

Help me remember that You are the God who provided food for the hungry crowds, and You certainly have enough of everything I need! Grant me joyful obedience, God. Sustain me through Your Spirit, who lives in me. Direct me down the right paths as I aim to deny myself, take up my cross, and follow You.

I surrender my life to You, Lord—every moment of my day, each decision I make, I yield my will and way to Your perfect will and way.

I love You too. Amen.

Rest, Catch Up, or Dig Deeper

 **WEEKLY CHALLENGE**

In Mark 7:31–37, Jesus healed a man who was deaf and had a speech impediment, and that man used his newfound voice to spread the good news about Jesus! This week, we'll aim to imitate that man by telling what God has done for us. In your journal, write down at least one way you saw God working or moving each day. Beside each entry, name at least one person you're going to tell about what God did. Use this opportunity as a tool to open your eyes and ears to the ways God is moving in your life that you otherwise might miss. When you begin to notice all the good God is up to in your life, share it as an encouragement to those around you!

Mark 9:
The Deity of the Servant

┌─ Scripture to Memorize ─┐

And many rebuked him, telling him to be silent. But he cried out all the more, "Son of David, have mercy on me!"

Mark 10:48

DAILY BIBLE READING

Day 1: Mark 9:1–13

Day 2: Mark 9:14–29

Day 3: Mark 9:30–37

Day 4: Mark 9:38–41

Day 5: Mark 9:42–50

Day 6: Psalm 94

Day 7: Catch-Up Day

Corresponds to Day 294 of *The Bible Recap*.

WEEKLY CHALLENGE

See page 169 for more information.

Mark 9:1–13

READ MARK 9:1-13

While they were still at Caesarea Philippi, the wicked site of pagan worship, Jesus foretold His death and resurrection. He promised that some of the people present would see the "kingdom of God after it has come with power." Many believe He was referring to the three disciples who would witness His transfiguration, which happened shortly afterward. It's the next scene in Mark's gospel.

For roughly a week, the disciples dealt with the news that their leader was going to be killed and resurrected from the dead. We can guess they felt confused and even disappointed that the Messiah they'd been following wasn't going to overthrow the government or give Israelites power, as they'd probably assumed. On the contrary, He was coming to be a suffering servant for all people. So Jesus took Peter, James, and John to the top of a high mountain to be witnesses as He was transfigured before them. These disciples experienced the full deity of Christ, and they were in awe as His clothes became whiter than anything they'd ever seen.

1. **Review 9:3–4.** How does Mark describe Jesus's appearance?

2. Why do you think Elijah and Moses were chosen to appear with Jesus?
Look up Exodus 24:1 and 1 Kings 19:8 for help.

Surely the disciples were shocked at the appearance of these two prophets, and they were either introduced to them or somehow divinely recognized them despite never having seen them before. Moses, being the giver of the law, represented the laws of Israel. Elijah, a well-known prophet, represented all the prophets of the Old Testament. In that moment, Jesus showed that He is both the fulfillment of the law and exactly who the prophets had spoken about. He also showed that the law and prophets have to give way to Jesus—He ultimately had power and dominion over them. Once again, Jesus proved that He was exactly who He had been telling them He was: the Son of God.

Peter was the first to speak. He was so in awe that he wanted to stay there in this literal mountaintop experience; he offered to prepare tents for Jesus, Elijah, and Moses. Since Peter was the one who rebuked Jesus six days ago for predicting His death, it's understandable that he wanted to prolong this moment as long as possible.

3. Put yourself in Peter's shoes: What do you think your response to this experience would've been?

As if Jesus being transfigured in front of their eyes weren't enough, God took it a step further. In 9:7, we see one of three times in the New Testament when people heard the audible voice of God the Father. He declared that Jesus was His Son, then gave a command to listen to Him.

4. **Do a web search to find the other two times in the New Testament when God the Father's voice is heard audibly.** Note the Scripture references and what God said.

Three times God the Father audibly confirmed that Jesus was the one true Son of God, coming in divine glory. On the heels of the news of what was about to happen to Him, Jesus was kind to give Peter, James, and John confidence and hope through witnessing His transfiguration. With their own eyes, they saw the kingdom of God coming with power through Jesus, exactly like He'd promised roughly a week earlier.

5. When is it hard to believe God is who He says He is? How does this passage give you comfort?

On the way down the mountain, Jesus told them to keep quiet about what they'd seen. He didn't need crowds or notoriety to get in the way of His mission to suffer and die for His people. As they often did, the disciples had questions afterward about Him rising from the dead and what the scribes meant by Elijah coming first. In Matthew's account of the transfiguration (Matthew 17:10–13), Jesus acknowledged that the "Elijah" He was referring to was JTB, who had come and prepared a way for the Messiah, fulfilling that prophecy.

In Jesus's glorified form, Peter, James, and John got a preview of His coming glorification as the true King of kings. These disciples, who had only known Him in His human body, now had a greater realization of the deity of Christ, even though they couldn't fully comprehend it. Knowing what's to come, how kind Jesus was to give them this assurance before He went to the cross!

6. Describe one or two of the ways God has revealed Himself to you. Be as specific and personal as you'd like. Then thank Him for it!

Mark 9:14–29

READ MARK 9:14–29

Coming down from the Mount of Transfiguration, Jesus encountered a crowd, including scribes who were arguing with the other disciples. A man had asked the disciples to try to heal his demon-possessed son, but they failed. The boy had suffered incredible pain and near-death experiences, and his father had grown desperate.

1. Fill out the table below documenting the ways the boy had been physically tormented by the unclean spirit.

9:17	
9:18	
9:20	
9:22	
9:25	
9:26	

It's obvious that the boy's possession had deeply impacted the lives of this father and son. Since the disciples had performed miracles before, it seems that both they and the father expected they'd be able to help the son. But they fell short. Jesus pressed the crowd—or perhaps just the disciples—about their lack of faith, which was apparently related to their lack of healing power.

Instead of giving up hope for healing, the father pressed on, asking Jesus if He could deliver what the disciples could not offer. Still, he was uncertain about God's power, His goodness, or both.

2. Even though God has been faithful and generous, we're quick to doubt His power and goodness. Describe one area of your life where you may be doubting the goodness and power of God in this season.

In his request, the father used a qualifier, saying, "*If* you can do anything." Jesus seized the opportunity to remind the boy's dad of His power, calling him to a higher level of faith.

3. Review 9:24. What does the father ask for? How do you identify with the father's request?

The father humbly acknowledged that while he did have faith, doubt was still mingled with his faith. Believing in the goodness of God while still wrestling with doubt is common in the Christian life. Even on our best days, our faith may be lacking. We can bring our requests to God with the pieces of faith we do possess and ask for more. And that's what the boy's dad did—instead of trying to hide his doubt or muster more faith on his own, he asked for help from the only One who could actually grant faith. And Jesus didn't rebuke him for asking for help—He healed the boy. Praise God that He still answers the prayers of imperfect people with imperfect faith!

Jesus also affirmed that all things are *possible* for those who believe in Him. This wasn't a guarantee that God will give us anything we ask for—it was a reminder to ask Him for the things we want and to believe that *He can*. Nothing is impossible for Him. Lack of ability is never the reason He answers some of our prayers with a no.

4. What big prayer have you avoided because you doubt God can answer with a yes?

Afterward, the disciples pulled Jesus aside to ask why they weren't able to heal the son on their own. Earlier in the story, Jesus pressed the crowd or the disciples about their lack of belief; it seems possible that the disciples had developed faith in *themselves* and were relying on their own abilities, rather than having faith in God and relying on His power. Their self-reliance seems to have prevented them from praying and asking God for help. Considering they had performed miracles before, it would've been easy to think, *I've got this*, and trust in their own abilities and experiences. It can be temping to want to access the power of God without involving the person of God.

5. Describe a scenario when you're tempted to act out of your own strength rather than a dependence on God.

Jesus clarified that prayer was a vital component in getting rid of the demon. Some ancient manuscripts of the book of Mark mention fasting in this verse as well. Prayer and fasting are two actions that mark a humble, dependent heart. They serve as evidence that we've put our faith in the right place, acknowledging that we can't do any good work without Him. Our faith is most evident in our commitment to and practice of prayer—it affirms our utter need for Him. When we submit to our desperate need for God, our rightly directed actions alongside rightly placed faith can do things that would otherwise be impossible.

6. Describe a time when you prayed and God answered with a yes.

Mark 9:30–37

🫙 READ MARK 9:30–37

In today's reading, Jesus predicted His own death for the second time. He reminded the disciples, preparing their hearts for what was about to take place. Today, we have the benefit of understanding His words because we know what happened, but the disciples were bewildered. Die and rise again? What could He mean by this? And why would He *keep* saying it, especially after their confusion and Peter's rebuke? Any time Jesus repeated information—especially to the same crowd—it's worth taking note. He was certain of what He was saying. He knew this was the Father's plan. His repetition confirms His confidence.

1. **Look up Revelation 13:8.** Where was it written that the Lamb would be slain?

2. When was it written?

Christ's death and resurrection had been the plan since before the foundation of the world. Jesus's life wasn't taken from Him, but willingly laid down. He knew and allowed everything that was going to take place. His use of the word *delivered* (9:31) hints at the Father's purposeful timing.

Being confused about His promise of a resurrection, the disciples likely assumed He was talking about the resurrection of all mankind at the end of the age. But instead of asking any questions, they kept quiet. They knew He was the Messiah but didn't seem to understand the necessity of His death or what the resurrection would mean. They could only see that He wasn't going to step in as a political liberator to set Israel free from Rome. So perhaps they understood enough of what Jesus was saying to know that they were scared—or dreading—to hear the rest of the details. It wasn't the picture-perfect ending they were hoping for.

Or perhaps they missed the magnitude of His words entirely. While Jesus was busy talking about laying down His life to serve and to save, they were arguing over who among them would be the greatest. How ironic!

Last week, we saw that every time Jesus predicted His own death and resurrection, He followed it with a teaching about discipleship, and this instance was no exception.

3. How did the disciples respond when Jesus asked what they were arguing about?

They were immediately ashamed of their conversation topic. Directly after hearing how their Messiah was going to humble Himself and lay down His life, they were fighting about power and positions. Even knowing the massive lengths Jesus was about to go for them, they couldn't see past their pride. Instead of rebuking them for their selfish heart postures, Jesus took a seat. In ancient Israel, the seated position was the official position of a teacher. It signaled, "Listen up! What I'm about to say matters, and I want you to listen and act on it."

4. Review 9:35. Write Jesus's statement in your own words.

Jesus took a child in His lap, defying the social standards of the day. Children were viewed as a nuisance until they could contribute to society. Juxtaposing kingdom values and the disciples' hearts, He said that whoever received the child received Him. Being a "servant to all" meant that not even the children were overlooked. Going one step further, He said that those who are considered great in the kingdom of heaven care for those who don't offer them status or anything else in return—like the child. The goal is not fame and power, but humility and service. Jesus said this heart attitude was the path to connection with the Father.

5. What is one way you can serve someone with less status than you today?

A heart of service doesn't mean you can't have ambition or drive. It doesn't even mean you can't accomplish big things in your life, but Jesus is after your heart posture. If you pursue big goals with the sole intent of greatness or power, it can reveal pride in your heart. When we depend on Jesus and His finished work on the cross, we can see ourselves rightly—desperately in need of a Savior. From there, we can begin to see and serve others from a place of gratitude and love. Jesus was the perfect example as He humbled Himself to be the ultimate "servant of all." Because of His willingness to become lowly, we are heirs of God and coheirs with Christ Himself!

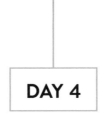
Mark 9:38–41

 READ MARK 9:38–41

When the disciples saw someone who wasn't in Jesus's inner circle casting out demons, they alerted Jesus about it. John said they'd tried to put a stop to it since the man wasn't one of the disciples, probably thinking Jesus would be proud of them for their vigilance. Instead, their pride showed through once again as they tried to silence someone they perceived as an outsider. Jesus had granted His disciples the power to cast out demons, but they were shocked to find that someone outside their immediate crew was able to do the same things.

1. In whose name was the man casting out demons?

This appeared to be a true believer in Jesus as the Messiah, and there are a few supporting bits of evidence for that idea. First, it seems like he was actually successful in casting out demons—something a magician or false prophet wouldn't be able to do. Second, he was casting them out in Jesus's name. In 9:39, Jesus affirmed that the man was indeed performing these miracles in His name.

2. Why would the disciples try to stop someone performing miracles in Jesus's name?

The disciples' actions reveal their assumption that the power to perform miracles was only granted to the twelve traveling with Jesus. It seems they wanted to be an elite group—the only ones who had access to the power of Christ. If we're not careful, we can get so narrowly focused on how we live out our faith that it can become easy to assume anything outside our group or comfort zone is not to be trusted.

The disciples thought they were protecting the ministry of Jesus, but Jesus's response tells us otherwise. Jesus said they shouldn't have stopped the man, because he was casting out demons in His name. If the man was able to call upon the name of Jesus, he wouldn't be able to then immediately denounce His name. This man was surely not a threat, but a member of the kingdom of God, walking in the power of Christ.

3. **Look up 1 Corinthians 12:3.** How does this verse strengthen Jesus's words in 9:39?

Jesus told His disciples that whoever was not against Him was for Him. In other words, there would be those who were part of His kingdom who weren't part of their immediate group. Today, Christians disagree on many issues that have caused divisions in the church and across denominations. This doesn't automatically mean one view is right and the other is wrong—some issues are matters of opinion. Yet Jesus wasn't saying that every protective wall should come down for the sake of unity. His words do provide a warning, however, to those who are quick to build walls where none are needed. The highest walls should be built around the primary doctrines—teachings that are considered foundational to the faith.

4. **In a trusted Bible study resource, look up the word** *doctrine.* **Define** it below in your own words.

5. **Using a dictionary or other resource, define** *primary, secondary,* **and** *tertiary issues* **as they apply to Christianity.**

Primary issues

Secondary issues

Tertiary issues

6. Choosing from the list below, write the letters corresponding to two issues in the primary ring, two in the secondary ring, and two in the tertiary ring. **Use your church's Statement of Beliefs (it may be on their website) for help.**

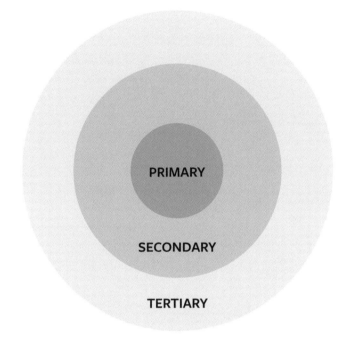

A. Jesus as the Son of God	G. Baptism practices
B. The Trinity	H. Formal attire at church
C. Women in church leadership	I. Salvation doctrine
D. End times timeline	J. Hymn / worship music style
E. Charismatic gifts today	K. Scripture is the inspired Word of God
F. Communion practices	

7. Are there areas in the list above (or other areas of your faith) where you have found yourself treating a secondary or tertiary issue as though it were primary? Describe below.

Scripture gives clear teaching on many things that we hold as absolutely true, but just because they are clear, that doesn't make them an absolute doctrine. For instance, it's clear in Scripture that Jesus wore a prayer shawl—it's the part of His garment that the woman touched when she was healed in Matthew 9:20. However, knowing and believing this detail isn't foundational to our faith.

It's important that we gain clarity on what issues are primary or secondary, and we must take care not to break unity over something that is nonessential. We also can't discriminate based on the perceived worth of someone's works or actions. Whether you're casting out demons or simply providing a cup of water to someone in need, Jesus said you will not lose your reward. God is glorified by every genuine act of faith in Christ. We need discernment to guide us in all these areas as we aim to walk in unity as the church.

8. Write a brief prayer below asking God for discernment.

DAY 5

Mark 9:42–50

🏺 READ MARK 9:42–50

Today's reading opened with a call to be mindful of how our actions can influence and impact others. In this section, Jesus used hyperbole to get His message across, making His point with startling clarity.

When He used the phrase *little ones*, Jesus wasn't necessarily talking exclusively about children. The term could also apply to a new believer or someone with childlike faith. And Jesus said it would be better to die than to cause one of them to sin.

1. What was the average weight of a millstone in the first century?

In the ancient world, a millstone was used to grind up grain to make flour. No human was strong enough to lift or move this stone on their own. It required a big animal, such as an ox, to move it so that it could grind the grain. Jesus used this harsh imagery to show the severity of the point He was trying to make. His choice of words reveals how much He wants to nurture the faith of those who are weak, vulnerable, and less knowledgeable than seasoned believers. We are called to live authentic lives in which our actions match our words and beliefs. It would be a tragedy for new believers to follow us down the path of sin or become confused by our inconsistency!

2. Take a moment to examine your life. Is there anything that would confuse or mislead a new believer?

Jesus went on to use the images of hands, feet, and eyes as things worthy to be cut off or plucked out in an effort to not sin. In Jewish culture, the hands, feet, and eyes were considered gifts from God, so the idea of intentionally desecrating a gift from God was another stark reminder of how seriously Jesus takes sin.

3. Look up Leviticus 19:28. What does it say about purposefully disfiguring your body?

4. Look up 2 Samuel 5:8. Who is not allowed in the temple?

The Torah prohibited the Jews from disfiguring their bodies in any way, and they weren't allowed to enter the temple if they had physical disfigurements. Yet Jesus said, as precious as those body parts were, it would be better to break the law, never set foot in the temple, and live without an important body part than to be cast into hell.

Again, these are strong images to convey His point. If you used your hand to steal, Jesus wasn't suggesting you literally cut it off. He was saying that whatever is precious to you—whether it's money, relationships, power, or status—is not worth having as much as the kingdom of God. Whatever keeps us from deeper intimacy with Him is something we should uproot from our lives.

5. Are there any sins you've diminished or ignored and haven't properly uprooted?

6. In a Greek lexicon, look up the word *hell* (9:47) and write its definition.

The word *gehenna* is related to a geographical location outside of Jerusalem. During the time of the Old Testament, many people participated in human and child sacrifices, and Gehenna was the designated location for sacrificing to the false god Molech. During King Josiah's reign, he wanted to desecrate this place to put an end to those sacrifices, so he turned it into a garbage dump for all of Jerusalem. The Jews would dump any and all trash—including feces, waste, and the carcasses of both animals and humans—on this pile that was constantly burning. The more they dumped on the pile, the more fuel the fire had, so they never had to relight it. Worms would eat the carcasses; and in this passage, Jesus said the worms do not die, meaning they would always have something to eat. This was the horrific imagery Jesus used to describe hell.

7. Does this change or give more clarity to your view of hell? If so, how?

This teaching gave severity not only to the weight of sin, but also to the weight of hell. Jesus used strong metaphors and language to drive His point home: Sin was to be avoided at any cost. Anything that would put you in the unquenchable fire and keep you from eternity with Christ wasn't worth it.

After such graphic imagery, Jesus pivoted to a different kind of fire. He had referred to fire as an unquenchable, horrible thing associated with hell, but fire is also a purifying force. Salt has purifying qualities too—it's used to clean, preserve, and give flavor. In 9:49, Jesus seems to use this imagery to say that the disciples weren't immune to being purified. Even though their eternal destiny was fixed, they weren't immune to the hardships of this life that would sanctify them.

8. Using a Bible study tool, look up the word *sanctification* and describe how it is related to the imagery of salt and fire.

Salt is used to preserve food and to give it flavor. However, if salt loses its saltiness, there's no real use for it. Jesus charged the disciples to be like salt. His words could be interpreted in two ways. First, He could've been calling them to "preserve" the Word and His teachings, to preach and teach in a way that wouldn't lead to false inputs or interpretations. Second, He could've been telling His disciples to "add flavor" to life in this world, to let their message and their actions enrich the world around them and show the beauty of living a set-apart life with Christ. When believers live in a way that reflects God's goodness and grace, they demonstrate the difference Jesus can make in someone's life for the better—because He's where the joy is!

9. What stood out to you most in this week's study? Why?

10. What did you learn or relearn about God and His character this week?

DAY 6

Corresponding
Psalm & Prayer

 **READ PSALM 94**

1. What correlation do you see between Psalm 94 and this week's study of Jesus and His kingdom?

2. What portions of this psalm stand out to you most?

3. Close by praying this prayer aloud:

Father,
    I praise You for Your righteous vengeance. I'm so grateful You're a God who punishes the wicked in just measures. And I'm grateful

that You lovingly discipline me when I've wandered off Your path. You can be trusted to do what is right.

I confess that I've despaired at times—I've felt like there was no hope for me. I confess that I've viewed Your loving discipline as wrathful punishment, and I've doubted Your love for me or Your goodness. And I confess that I've ignored sins in my life because I loved them, or because they didn't seem to hurt anyone else, or because I didn't think it was possible to overcome them. But I know that with You, all things are possible. I repent of my sins and turn to You instead—the only one who can make my heart clean. Lord, I believe. Help my unbelief.

Continue to sanctify me. Show me what things are most important to You, and direct my heart toward Your priorities. Protect me from the attacks of the enemy, God. You are stronger, and Your Spirit lives in me, so I trust that I have everything I need when temptations and trials come my way. Comfort me in my aches. Teach me Your ways. When I'm tempted to forget, remind me that You are my safe place.

I surrender my life to You, Lord—every moment of my day, each decision I make, I yield my will and way to Your perfect will and way.

I love You too. Amen.

Rest, Catch Up, or Dig Deeper

 **WEEKLY CHALLENGE**

On Day 4, we discussed what classifies as primary, secondary, and tertiary issues within Christianity. Let's find out a bit more about what various churches believe in each of these areas. First, go to your home church's website and look up their statement of beliefs to see what they consider of primary importance. (It's worth noting that many churches only list their primary beliefs.) Next, do the same with another church in another city. And finally, do the same with a church that belongs to a different Christian denomination. What do you notice that is consistent? What do you notice that is different? How does this inform or challenge your views on primary, secondary, and tertiary issues within the Christian faith?

─ Scripture to Memorize ─

And Jesus stopped and said, "Call him." And they called the blind man, saying to him, "Take heart. Get up; he is calling you."

Mark 10:49

Mark 10–11:
The Purpose of the Servant

DAILY BIBLE READING

Day 1: Mark 10:1–31
Day 2: Mark 10:32–52
Day 3: Mark 11:1–11
Day 4: Mark 11:12–25
Day 5: Mark 11:27–33
Day 6: Psalm 145
Day 7: Catch-Up Day

Corresponds to Days 304 and 307 of *The Bible Recap*.

WEEKLY CHALLENGE

See page 194 for more information.

Mark 10:1–31

 **READ MARK 10:1–31**

Today's reading touched on some topics that are potentially raw and difficult. But Jesus didn't shy away from these topics, so we can't either. Jesus left His home base of Capernaum one last time on His journey to celebrate Passover in Jerusalem. When He arrived in the region of Judea, the crowds gathered, and He taught them. This time, the Pharisees pulled no punches. They wanted to talk about a hotly debated topic: divorce.

In many ancient cultures, a man could divorce his wife for any minor issue, and some cultures even morally obligated him to it. The Pharisees seemed to assume Jesus would have to either speak against the popular opinion or prohibit divorce altogether—and either answer would cause the crowd to turn on Him. Jesus skillfully put the question back on the Pharisees by asking what Moses commanded.

1. **Read Deuteronomy 24:1–4.** Did Moses *command* divorce or did he *permit* divorce? Why is the distinction important?

Jesus's question gives us helpful insight. Moses never commanded divorce, but he did make a concession for it. Divorce was permitted, within certain parameters, because of the fall. God's desire was for the perfect unity and harmony of the people bearing His image. His aim was for good and for blessing.

2. How do you think the Pharisees might have responded to Jesus's answer?

The disciples genuinely wanted to learn from Jesus, so they asked Him about it in private. Often, when Jesus had a private conversation with His disciples after talking to a large crowd, He switched into a higher gear. He offered a more straightforward response to His followers, as opposed to the cynics and critics who didn't truly want to understand.

In 10:11–12, Jesus spoke some of His most challenging words. In fact, in Matthew's account of this conversation (Matthew 19:8–11), the disciples seemed so taken aback by His teaching that they said it might be better to never marry. Though we are sinful, fallen people, God's design was perfect, and we are to pursue holiness. There is hope for us because of what Jesus accomplished on the cross! When sin rears its ugly head in our lives, 1 John 1:9 says confession and repentance put us back into alignment with Him.

3. Review 10:13–16. Why might the disciples rebuke the parents?

As we saw in the last chapter (9:36–37), children weren't rightly valued. It was a cultural norm to treat them dismissively, and talking with them would've been considered a waste of a rabbi's time. But Jesus continued to reveal that He came to serve *everyone*. Jesus pointed out the beauty of the kids' enthusiasm and lack of cynicism—especially obvious when contrasted with the Pharisees' attitude. The kingdom of God is for those who love God and are excited to draw near to Him—just like the kids did!

4. **Review 10:17.** How would you expect Jesus to answer the man's question?

The man we often refer to as "The Rich Young Man" urgently and respectfully approached Jesus with one of the most important questions anyone can ask. But even in his question, he revealed a misunderstanding of the kingdom. In Jesus's reply (10:18), He wasn't denying His deity—He was pushing the man to reflect on the meaning of his own words.

"What must I do to inherit eternal life?" seems to assume eternal life is inherited by doing good deeds. This perspective is still at the forefront of theology today. A 2020 study found that 52 percent of professing Christians in America believe that God's acceptance comes through their works.*

Amazingly, instead of rebuking the man's obvious misunderstanding of his own sin, Jesus's heart was filled with compassion. The man claimed to have kept all the commandments, but Jesus pointed out that his real problem wasn't his actions but his heart. He clung to his riches above all else. Jesus said it was impossible for anyone to depend on their wealth while also recognizing their spiritual poverty.

Jesus didn't say wealth is bad but that it isn't *ultimate*. Scripture introduces us to many wealthy people who used their God-given resources to glorify God. Lydia (Acts 16:14–15), Joseph (Genesis 41:41–43, 56–57), the Shunammite woman (2 Kings 4:8–10), and Joseph of Arimathea (Matthew 27:57–60) all stand out as people whose wealth belonged to the kingdom.

Peter pointed out that he'd left everything to follow Jesus, and Jesus affirmed that eternal life is for all who are willing to sacrifice everything for

*"American Worldview Inventory 2020 – At a Glance," Cultural Research Center, Arizona Christian University, https://www.arizonachristian.edu/wp-content/uploads/2020/08/AWVI-2020-Release-08-Perceptions-of-Sin-and-Salvation.pdf.

the sake of the gospel. But He also acknowledged something that many of us would prefer to skip over: the accompanying promise of persecution.

5. How might you need to reorient your own thinking about wealth based on what you've learned?

Mark 10:32–52

READ MARK 10:32-52

On the uphill path to Jerusalem, the mood was astonishment mixed with fear. Ostensibly, they were on their way to celebrate a religious festival, but Jesus gave His disciples a clear picture of the emotional and physical suffering He would endure as He died—but He promised to rise again. For the disciples, this defied understanding.

1. **Read Isaiah 9:6–7 and Jeremiah 23:4–6.** Based on these passages and the fact that first-century Jews were under Roman rule, what do you think most people were looking for in the prophesied Messiah?

In the minds of many, this long-awaited savior would be a military ruler who would defeat their oppressors and protect Israel from the surrounding nations. They were looking for salvation from human opposition, not for eternal salvation of their souls. Their desires were far too short-sighted. James and John confirmed this mindset when they asked Jesus for a favor.

2. **Look up 10:37–40 in a Bible commentary.** Summarize this section in your own words.

The request was a gross underestimation of the kingdom and overestimation of their abilities. Jeremiah 25:15 speaks of a cup that represents the wrath of God. James and John seem to think that they were able to face the same wrath He would have to endure, earning them seats of importance in His kingdom. Interestingly, Jesus told them that they *would* face the suffering and persecution of being associated with Him but that the positions of honor were not up for grabs.

3. Do you ever see a glory-grabbing mindset in your own life? If so, describe what it can look like.

Jesus contrasted the world's values of power and authority with the kingdom values of service and humility. And in 10:45, He gives one of the clearest purpose statements about His life on earth. His life had two goals: to serve, then to give His life as a ransom for many. Jesus modeled for His followers that ministry wasn't about what the minister gained but about what was given. And in His most demonstrative act of service, He *willingly gave* His life for many—it wasn't taken from Him.

4. Read the passages below and fill out the chart.

Verse	What did Jesus do?	How were people served?
Romans 5:10		
1 Peter 3:18		
1 Corinthians 15:3–8		
2 Corinthians 5:21		
Isaiah 53:1–12		
Colossians 2:13–14		

Believers identify with Jesus's suffering because He was the one who stood in the place of guilty sinners and offered Himself as a substitute on their behalf. Theologically speaking, this is referred to as penal substitutionary atonement. Mankind is separated from God and deserves His wrath due to our sin. But we can receive salvation instead of the punishment we deserve! Jesus, who is fully God and fully man, stepped in as the substitute for all those (the "many" of 10:45) who will receive it.

As Jesus and His followers entered Jericho on their way to Jerusalem, they encountered a poor blind man who had a better grasp of Jesus's messianic message than His closest disciples. When he heard that Jesus was approaching, Bartimaeus couldn't be silenced in his plea for Jesus's attention. It seems he may have known Jesus was the Messiah, because he called Jesus the "Son of David"—a reference to Jeremiah 23:5 and 2 Samuel 7:12–16. When Jesus stopped and asked for Bartimaeus to be brought to Him, Bartimaeus sprang up.

5. Are you quick to respond when Jesus calls to you?

The question Jesus asked Bartimaeus is the same question He asked James and John: "What do you want me to do for you?" But where James and John answered with hints of greed, pride, and an overestimation of their abilities, Bartimaeus responded humbly.

6. Look up the word *rabbi* (10:51) in a Greek lexicon. Where is the only other place this version of Jesus's title (*rabboni*) is used? How is it different from other uses of the word *rabbi*?

This form of the word is tender and personal, and it's also viewed as a confession of faith. Bartimaeus asked for only one thing: healing. He didn't ask for status—he asked for freedom from darkness. Jesus granted the request and told Bartimaeus to go on his way because his faith had made him well. After immediately recovering his sight, Bartimaeus didn't go on *his* way, he followed Jesus on *the* way!

Mark 11:1–11

 **READ MARK 11:1–11**

This passage of Mark is filled with symbolism and prophetic fulfillment, giving a picture of the heart and values of Jesus.

1. **Locate Bethphage and Bethany on the map.** How long is the walk from each village to Jerusalem?

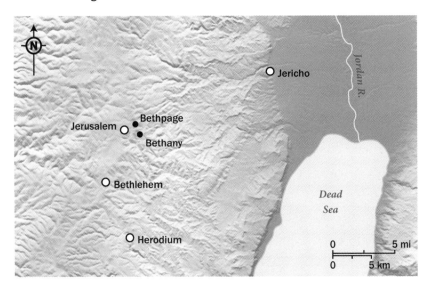

Jesus was walking out a perfectly timed plan; His entry into Jerusalem was not left to chance. He sent two disciples on a very specific errand and even gave them a script to follow. He requested a colt that had never been ridden. Climbing onto the back of an unbroken animal for the first time seems like an odd choice at first, but we don't know the details of this trip. Perhaps Jesus showed His authority over all things and the colt moved calmly—or maybe He had a difficult ride!

2. Read Zechariah 9:9. How did Jesus fulfill this prophecy?

The custom of the day was for a ruler, king, or victorious warrior to triumphantly ride a large horse or stallion into his city after a great victory. This was a display of might and authority. Jesus, on the other hand, rode an unbroken colt. He wasn't escorted by His armies or prestigious advisors but by a group of average Galileans who had chosen to follow Him.

3. Read the accounts of the triumphal entry in the other three gospels (Matthew 21:1–11; Luke 19:28–42; John 12:12–19). What other details do you notice in these accounts? List one piece of information from each of the three that helps fill out the picture.

Matthew 21:1–11	Luke 19:28–42	John 12:12–19

When Jesus began His ride down Mount Olives toward Jerusalem, the people began worshiping Him physically and verbally. Each of their actions and words was full of meaning.

4. **Review 11:8–10.** What three things did the people do to worship Jesus on His way toward Jerusalem?

A 2020 survey suggested that the average person owns 148 pieces of clothing.* Due to the relative poverty of the average person in Jesus's day, most people had only one cloak. The people worshiping Jesus took off their cloaks and laid them on a dusty road. The leafy branches (John's gospel tells us they're palm branches) symbolized political strength and military victory. And the shouts of worship weren't random—they were rich with hopeful expectation.

5. **Look up the word *hosanna* (11:9) in a Hebrew lexicon.** What were the people asking Jesus to do?

6. **Read Psalm 118:25–29.** How did the shouts of the people partially fulfill this messianic psalm?

* *"Global Fashion Industry Statistics," Fashion United, https://fashionunited.com/global-fashion-industry-statistics.

The people were shouting a plea for salvation. They seemed to recognize the messianic nature of Jesus's presence, since they invoked the kingdom of David in their worship. They worshiped Jesus by shouting the words of Scripture *about* Jesus back *to* Jesus!

7. Why is using Scripture as worship powerful or meaningful?

8. Make a list of worship songs you know that pull lyrics directly from Scripture.

In fulfillment of Malachi 3:1, when Jesus got to Jerusalem, He went into the temple and looked around—taking in everything, perhaps surveying it for what He will do in tomorrow's reading. Then He walked back to Bethany with His disciples. This may seem like an underwhelming verse, but nothing about this passage is anticlimactic. The God of the universe had just entered Jerusalem for the final week of His life. This Savior Servant didn't come as a conquering general or a powerful ruler, but with humility, on the back of a colt. In this scene, Jesus allowed and received public pronouncements of His fulfillment of the messianic promise for the first time! He fulfilled Old Testament prophecies and headed back to Bethany knowing what awaited Him in the days ahead.

Mark 11:12–25

READ MARK 11:12–25

Jesus was hungry as He walked the two miles from Bethany back to the temple, and He saw a fig tree in the distance. In 11:13, Mark tells us that the tree was "in leaf" but that "it was not the season for figs."

Some scholars believe Jesus used this tree as an illustration for hypocrisy—cursing a tree that *appeared* to have fruit ("in leaf") but that didn't. If this is the case, it was an appropriate illustration for the Pharisees, whom Jesus repeatedly called hypocrites.

Other scholars lean into the part of 11:13 that says "it was not the season for figs"—something Jesus would've been aware of, having lived in an agrarian society all of His life. In this view, Jesus didn't expect the tree to have figs, but cursed the tree to demonstrate His grief over Israel's lack of fruit.

1. Given what you know, which interpretation do you prefer and why?

Regardless of the interpretation, God's heart for His people was on full display, so what Jesus did next comes as no surprise. Jesus had been in the temple the evening before, surveying His surroundings, and He came back to act on what He saw.

2. **Review 11:15–16.** List the four actions Jesus took.

3. **Review 11:17.** What two terms did Jesus use to describe the temple?

In one of His references, Jesus quoted Isaiah 56:7. God has always had a heart for people of *all* nations, and the temple was the place where that love should've been most on display. There was even an area called the Court of the Gentiles, established for all non-Jews.

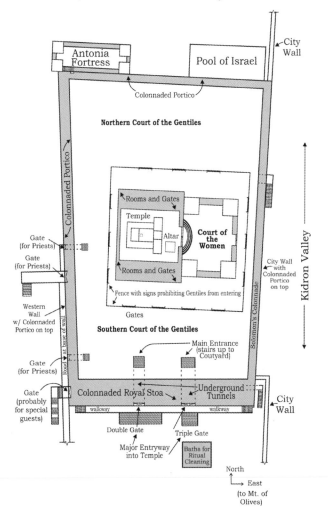

People came to the temple from great distances and needed to make sacrifices when they arrived. Traveling with an animal and hoping it would remain blemish-free was unrealistic, so those selling animals were providing a much-needed service. However, their business practices were unfair and corrupt—which is why Jesus called them robbers. They had a reputation for price gouging the poor and the tourists. They had turned God's house into a place that served their own purposes instead of a place of service for all peoples. Those who came to the temple to obey God were being hindered by the very people who were supposed to help them draw near to God!

4. **Review 11:18.** How did the crowd respond to Jesus's teaching? How did the chief priests and the scribes respond?

On their way out of the city, Jesus and the disciples passed the same fig tree that had been in full leaf the previous day. Peter pointed out that the fig tree had completely withered.

5. **Review 11:22–24.** How might this passage be used wrongly if taken out of context?

6. Read the following passages and summarize what each says about prayer.

Romans 8:26–28

James 5:16

1 Thessalonians 5:16–19

John 15:7–11

Jeremiah 29:12–13

1 John 5:14–15

Psalm 145:17–19

James 1:5–8

Faith in God doesn't mean we get whatever we want. Faith in God is knowing that His goodness and sovereignty will work together for our good and His glory. It also means praying *expectantly* for the things God already promised in Scripture. This requires humility and submission to the will of God, not a focus on ourselves.

Jesus finished His comments about faith and prayer with a command and a reminder. Keep in mind that Jesus wasn't giving a full teaching on the theology of forgiveness—He was connecting it to what He'd just finished teaching about faith.

7. How can unforgiveness be a hindrance to faith and prayer?

8. Describe a time when unforgiveness or bitterness kept you from faithful prayer.

Jesus reminded His disciples that boundless forgiveness was available to them and that forgiving others was part of having faith in God.*

*We're ending today's reading with verse 25 and starting tomorrow's reading with verse 27, and that's on purpose! Many translations don't include Mark 11:26 because scholars have concluded this verse was not written by Mark but was added to later manuscripts.

Mark 11:27–33

 **READ MARK 11:27–33**

Even though the chief priests and scribes sought to destroy Jesus for driving out the money changers and turning over tables, He returned. The leaders met Him there and asked Him who authorized Him to do such things—in other words, "*Who sent you?*"

The scribes and Pharisees often asked Jesus questions in an effort to trap Him or turn the crowds against Him. Jesus skillfully pulled a similar move, turning the tables on them. In front of the crowds, He asked them about the well-known, much-revered JTB.

1. Review 11:31–32. What does their internal dialogue reveal about their primary motives?

On the surface, they feared the revolt of the people. But on an even deeper level, they knew that if JTB's baptism was from heaven, then what he said about Jesus must also be true. They weren't motivated by a desire for the truth, but by self-preservation and maintaining the status quo.

2. Have you ever tried to avoid the truth—either hearing it or speaking it—as an act of self-preservation? Describe the impact it had on you (emotionally, spiritually, physically, etc.).

Instead of answering Jesus with intellectual integrity and humility, they answered with a lie: "We do not know." And because they weren't engaging Jesus to pursue truth, Jesus simply refused to engage with them.

3. Read John 3:17–21. How does the truth in this passage impact the way you view and approach God?

Our sovereign and all-knowing God was not surprised by the lies of the religious leaders, because He knew their thoughts. This can be an overwhelming reality—that God knows our thoughts—but only if we view Him as one who is waiting to strike us down for every mistake or sin. But because of God's great love for those who bear His image, Jesus came to seek and save the lost and broken! He asks that we come to Him fully acknowledging our brokenness and need for Him—renouncing the lie of our self-sufficiency. He came to serve those who cannot serve themselves.

Jesus defied expectations for a leader in the first century. He was humble, wouldn't respond to provocations, rode into the city on a colt, and encouraged His followers to forgive. All these things demonstrate the heart of the One who came to serve and give His life as a ransom for many. He demonstrated that the path to joy is through humble service, and He invites us to follow Him on that path, because He's where the joy is!

4. What stood out to you most in this week's study? Why?

5. What did you learn or relearn about God and His character this week?

DAY 6

Corresponding Psalm & Prayer

 **READ PSALM 145**

1. What correlation do you see between Psalm 145 and this week's study of Jesus and His kingdom?

2. What portions of this psalm stand out to you most?

3. Close by praying this prayer aloud:

Father,

You deserve my praise forever, God! You are my King, and I bless Your name. No matter how many times I praise You, I will never capture all the goodness of who You are. You're merciful—You spare me the punishment I deserve. You're gracious—You give me blessings I could never earn. Your steadfast love abounds to me! Every single thing You do isn't just righteous—it's also kind. There is no one like You.

And unlike You, I'm a sinner. I confess that I've run from the truth like the scribes and the chief priests. I've been more concerned with self-preservation and earning the respect of others. Like James and John, I've tried to grab at glory for myself, but I do not deserve glory, God—You alone do. I confess that I've been like the rich young ruler at times—elevating my obedience too highly and esteeming You too lowly. Sometimes my possessions have been a distraction to me, and I repent.

Will You change my heart, God? Give me a heart that loves You above all else, that seeks Your glory instead of my own. Give me a heart that loves the truth. Put my fear and self-preservation to death, and teach me to be a servant like Your Son, Jesus.

I surrender my life to You, Lord—every moment of my day, each decision I make, I yield my will and way to Your perfect will and way.

I love You too. Amen.

Rest, Catch Up, or Dig Deeper

WEEKLY CHALLENGE

As Jesus walked into Jerusalem a week before His death, the people worshiped Him by quoting Psalm 118. Some say the worship songs we sing are just as important as the sermons we listen to since they stay in our heads longer and they more often impact us on a heart level. John 4:24 says we must worship Him in Spirit and truth. Since God's Word is the ultimate source of truth, it makes sense that we would want our worship to be in alignment with the Bible. For this week's challenge, look up the lyrics of your favorite worship song. Using whatever resources you need, find the biblical support for the lyrics of the song and write them in your journal or on a printout of the lyrics. If you have difficulty, ask a pastor, worship leader, or trusted friend or mentor to help you.

Mark 12–13:
The Servant's Economy

DAILY BIBLE READING

Day 1: Mark 12:1–17

Day 2: Mark 12:18–34

Day 3: Mark 12:35–44

Day 4: Mark 13:1–23

Day 5: Mark 13:24–37

Day 6: Psalm 102

Day 7: Catch-Up Day

Corresponds to Days 308 and 310 of *The Bible Recap*.

WEEKLY CHALLENGE

See page 217 for more information.

Mark 12:1–17

READ MARK 12:1–17

When we left off at the end of chapter 11, Jesus and His disciples had been walking in the temple in Jerusalem. There, Jewish religious leaders had demanded that He answer a question amounting to "Who do You think You are?" After putting the leaders in their place, Jesus told them a story.

During His ministry, Jesus often used parables when He spoke to large crowds of common people. But when the religious leaders refused to answer Him (11:33), Jesus used a parable as a not-so-subtle indictment.

1. **Review 12:1–9.** Match the parable characters to who they represent.

Vineyard owner	Pharisees
Tenants	Jesus
Servants	God
Son	Prophets

When Jesus finished His parable, He made another theological point for the Pharisees. He asked them if they'd read Psalm 118:22–23, which says, "The stone that the builders rejected has become the cornerstone. This is the LORD's doing; it is marvelous in our eyes." Any time Jesus asked the Pharisees if they'd read Scripture, the answer was obviously that they had but didn't rightly understand what they'd read. They were too focused on establishing themselves as righteous to see that Jesus was the fulfillment of this Scripture.

2. What do you look for when you read Scripture?

3. How might this shape what you notice and what you miss?

The Pharisees had of course read Psalm 118. They knew it was a messianic psalm that pointed to the rejection of the Messiah by Israel's leaders—they disrespected and disregarded God's Son—much like the tenants in the parable. The psalm also prophesied the church's acceptance of the Son as God's heir, and His place as the cornerstone of the kingdom. While the religious leaders rejected Him, the people of the church He was building embraced Him.

The Pharisees felt the righteous sting of Jesus's charge, and they went away intent on finding a way to arrest Him.

In the next scene in Jerusalem's temple, the Pharisees came back, and this time, they teamed up with the Herodians. Herodians were a Jewish political group who approved of Herod's compromises with Rome.

Herodians and Pharisees rarely had anything to do with each other, but they managed to put aside their differences to unite behind their hatred of Jesus.

They set another trap in the form of a question wrapped up in flattery.

4. **Review 12:13–14.** How did the Pharisees and Herodians flatter Jesus?

5. What did they ask Him?

The Pharisees often tried to force Jesus to pit religion against Rome. If Jesus had answered yes to their question, it would've implied that He supported Roman rule, which oppressed the Jewish people. This was viewed by many as a compromised devotion to God. If Jesus had answered no to their question, it would've been seen as rebellion against Rome, and maybe even treason, which would be cause for arrest. In their minds, no matter how He answered, He would either disregard God's commands or subvert Rome's laws.

But as Jesus often did, He saw through their trap and responded with truth beyond what they'd asked Him in the first place. Then and now, every person bears God's image, and every person is held accountable to earthly laws. Christians around the world are called to submit ourselves to both temporary and eternal authority.

6. **Review 12:15–17 and read Genesis 1:27.** Then fill in the table below.

This . . .	is stamped with the image of . . .	so it belongs to . . .
Denarius		
Human		

Jesus's answer instructed the people to submit to authority: Rome's and God's. But He didn't equate the two; He ranked the authority rightly. Rome's authority didn't come close to God's. It was temporary, so even though it was right to submit to Rome's authority by paying taxes and following laws, it wouldn't last forever. But God's authority is forever. It's always right to submit to His authority, because it's supreme and eternal.

Mark 12:18–34

READ MARK 12:18–34

Still in the temple in Jerusalem, the Sadducees took their turn to lay a trap for Jesus. They asked Him about eternal life, which the Sadducees didn't even believe in. They only followed the Pentateuch—the first five books of the Bible—which the Sadducees claimed didn't have any teaching on eternal life.

The Sadducees centered their snare around one of the laws God had given His people to ensure the vulnerable were cared for.

1. **Read Deuteronomy 25:5.** What did this law say?

Jesus's questioners made up a story about a widow who was married seven times. They feigned concern for the hypothetical woman by asking if she would have seven husbands in heaven.

A note here: Jesus's response that there won't be human marriage in heaven may have made you feel uneasy. If you're married, maybe your marriage has been a picture of God's goodness to you. If you're single, maybe you've felt the sting of the lie that God is withholding His best gift from you. Take heart. No matter what our situation is here on earth, or whether our closest relationships have been a source of joy or pain, those relationships will be different in the next life. Heaven isn't an extension of this life, but rather a *new* life. Even the best, most beautiful gifts we have here will pale in comparison to what's waiting for us there as the bride of Christ!

The Sadducees' real question wasn't about their hypothetical widow or her marital status, anyway; their question was about the resurrection of the dead, which they denied. Since they claimed the Pentateuch had no teaching on eternal life, Jesus took them back there to a passage they would've known well and pointed out what they'd missed all along.

2. **Read Exodus 3:6.** Write what God said to Moses.

3. **Read Romans 8:38–39.** What is the first thing listed that *can't* separate us from the love of God?

In Exodus, God spoke about Abraham, Isaac, and Jacob as if they were still alive. Because they were, and they are! And one day, they will also be raised from the dead. Because God's loving covenant with His people extends beyond death, God always has been—and always will be—the God of the living.

Not all of the religious leaders in the temple who heard Jesus's teachings left angry. One scribe who had been listening intently had a wholly different response.

4. Review 12:28. What did the scribe think of Jesus's answers to the religious leaders? In your own words, write the scribe's question.

The scribe spent his days reading and copying Scripture. The Old Testament was full of God's laws—over six hundred of them. Some religious teachers insisted that every law was equally vital, but others made a hierarchy of which laws *really* needed to be followed, and which were okay to skip.

The scribe wanted to know: Which commandment is the most important? At the heart of the scribe's genuine inquiry is a question that God's kids have been wondering since the beginning of time: "How do I live a life that pleases God?" Do you ask yourself similar questions? *Why am I here and what should I do? How should I live? What is the chief end of man?* No matter how they're phrased, all of these questions ask about our purpose.

5. Read Matthew 22:35–40 and Luke 10:25–28. Then review Mark 12:29–31. What's different about Mark's account of Jesus's answer?

Only Mark includes Jesus's use of the Shema, a Jewish statement of faith from Deuteronomy 6:4. In Hebrew, *shema* comes from the word that means "hear," and even today, religious Jews repeat it twice daily. It is a vital component of Judaism. The Shema affirms the unity of God and God's covenant with Israel.

6. Why might Jesus have begun His answer to the scribe with the Shema? Use a Bible commentary if you need help.

7. What is the most important commandment according to Jesus?

8. What is the second?

A lightbulb turned on for the scribe, and he excitedly agreed that God's concern is for what's happening on the inside of a person, not just the outside. These two commandments don't exclude any or make a hierarchy of God's laws, but they summarize all of them. The scribe understood that obedience to God's laws comes from the heart, and Jesus affirmed his wisdom.

9. Which of these two commandments is the most challenging for you? Why?

Mark 12:35–44

READ MARK 12:35–44

Yesterday, our reading ended with "And after that no one dared to ask him any more questions" (12:34). Jesus had responded to everything asked of Him—whether it was a trap intended to incriminate or a question intended to clarify—with the wisdom and knowledge of God. And with the questioners left in silence, it was Jesus's turn to ask a question.

1. **Review Mark 12:35–37.**

Jesus asks if the Messiah is the *son* of David or the *Lord* of David. In Psalm 110, because the Holy Spirit was with him, David prophesied that the Messiah would not only be his son, but his Lord. Jesus wasn't denying that He was a descendant of David, but was rather explaining that He was also the Son of God.

2. **Read Romans 1:1–6.** How does Paul's summary of the gospel connect to David's psalm and Jesus's teaching?

Among the Jewish religious leaders of Jesus's time, there was widespread corruption and hard-heartedness. We just read yesterday that Jesus praised a scribe for his wisdom, but he was the exception to the rule. Religious leaders at the time received no official salary and were supported by the people they taught and led. The leaders were meant to serve and to be served in return.

The problem was that many of these religious leaders demanded a social status that exceeded their religious authority. So they neglected to serve, while at the same time exploiting the ones serving them. Jesus warned His followers to beware of them—it can be easy to be swayed by flashy things and forget that our Savior demonstrated a heart of service.

3. Review 12:38–40. According to Jesus, what are the five things these corrupt scribes did?

4. Read James 1:27. How does the list above compare to what James called "pure and undefiled" religion?

They were more concerned with their own status and appearance—praying long prayers not because they loved talking with God, but "out of pretense." Their focus on themselves left them no attention to devote to those in need. Jesus said the greater condemnation would be theirs—Scripture carries the theme that leaders are held to a higher standard. But instead of taking care of the needs of the vulnerable, the scribes took advantage. Meanwhile, one of the vulnerable gave everything she had.

5. **Review 12:41–44.** What did Jesus say about the widow's offering?

Jesus took time to notice and point out this woman—who stood in stark contrast to the religious leaders. Her actions demonstrated a heart of faith and generosity. Her focus was outward. And Jesus honored her.

In the gospel of Mark, from the widow's offering up until His arrest, Jesus spent His time away from the public, in the company of His disciples. After the corrupt leaders failed to trick Jesus, but before He retreated away from the crowds, Jesus showed His followers a beautiful picture of faith. We don't know what happened to the woman who gave everything she had, but we know the heart of Jesus, the One who gives everything we need. Because He gave His life, we gain ours. In His economy, giving a little in faith turns into so much more. And in His kingdom, the last are first.

6. Describe a time when giving sacrificially led to your joy.

DAY 4

Mark 13:1–23

 **READ MARK 13:1–23**

As Jesus and the disciples left the temple, one of them commented on the magnificence of the building. And it *was* magnificent! Under Herod's rule, the temple was expanded and beautifully adorned. It was an architectural and artistic masterpiece. But Jesus told them something that promptly killed the mood.

1. **Review 13:2.** In your own words, write what Jesus told the disciples about the temple.

As Jesus sat down on Mount Olives, Peter, James, John, and Andrew went to Him for clarification. We've seen this before: After Jesus made a public statement that was confusing or troubling, He would clarify His meaning for His disciples privately.

From their place on Mount Olives, just outside Jerusalem, Jesus and these four disciples saw an expansive view of Jerusalem and the temple. If you've ever seen your city from an airplane window or the top of a mountain at the end of a hike, hopefully you've found yourself momentarily awed, reflecting on thoughts and ideas bigger than yourself.

From their wide-angle view of the beautiful temple, Jesus said it would be destroyed. He was referring to the literal destruction of the temple that would happen not long after this time, during the first Jewish-Roman war in AD 70. We know now that this didn't usher in the end of time. But at that time, the disciples very likely equated Jesus's foretelling of the temple's destruction with the end of the age. So they asked Jesus two questions about the end times: When are these things going to happen? And how will we know when they've happened?

The remaining verses of this chapter contain some of the most theologically complex content we'll study in Mark. This passage is known as the Olivet Discourse—because it took place on Mount Olives—and in these verses we find Jesus's teachings on the end times.

2. What do the words *end times* make you feel? Anxiety, frustration, excitement, curiosity, something else?

3. Take a moment to stop and pray. Tell God how you feel and ask Him to be with you as you study His teaching on this topic.

4. Review 13:3–23. As you read, ask yourself these questions: A) Who is this message for? And B) What part of this message is information, and what part of this message is instruction?

We're living in what Galatians 1:4 calls the "present evil age," which will continue until the second coming of Christ. The things He listed as the "beginning of the birth pains" have been happening all along—wars, earthquakes, famines—which is why many previous generations have also had a sense that they were in the end times.

5. Review 13:6–13. List some of the "birth pains" that will mark the end times.

6. Review 13:14. Use a study Bible to define "abomination of desolation." Make sure to read Daniel 9:27, 11:31, and 12:11 before you define it.

Some theologians view the Antichrist's desecration of the temple as referring to the actual temple, which means that it happened almost two thousand years ago. Others take the view that the temple refers to the people of God, which means it's still to come. Using that framework, the tribulation that's coming will include some of the worst suffering since the beginning of creation. Jesus didn't sugarcoat this. But did you catch God's goodness in the midst of this passage that might bring fear?

7. Review 13:20. What will God do for His kids?

Jesus's response dealt primarily with the disciples' second question, talking about the signs of the end of the age instead of its timing. Information from God about events of the future should inform how we live in the present. If we occupy ourselves grasping at straws to make guesses about the timing of the end of the age, we will fail to live fully and righteously in the time we have now.

We'll continue studying the Olivet Discourse tomorrow. But with what we know so far, take a moment to answer the two questions you asked yourself while you studied.

8. Who is this message for?

9. What is information and what is instruction? In the verses below, underline the information and circle the instruction.

- "Many will come in my name, saying, 'I am he!' and they will lead many astray. And when you hear of wars and rumors of wars, do not be alarmed." (13:6–7)

- "For false christs and false prophets will arise and perform signs and wonders, to lead astray, if possible, the elect. But be on guard; I have told you all things beforehand." (13:22–23)

These words can feel scary and dark, but for those who know Christ, they are drenched in hope. When He returns, the time that creation has been longing for since the fall of man will begin, and all things will be made new!

Mark 13:24–37

 READ MARK 13:24–37

Continuing the Olivet Discourse, Jesus told His disciples that after the tribulation, things would change dramatically. Some theologians believe He was saying the forces of nature will shift and the cosmos will be transformed. Others believe He was using a metaphor for the political and religious authorities, who will fall from their positions of power when His return reveals His sovereign rule. Regardless of which view you hold, the underlying message remains the same: Creation will respond righteously to the extraordinary event when Christ the Creator, who came first in humility, comes again in glory!

1. **Review 13:24–27. Read Revelation 19:11–16. Then read Mark 11:1–11.** Fill in the chart below, noting details of the two events.

Triumphal Entry	Jesus's Return

After His disciples heard Jesus talk about the signs of the end of the age, the desecration of the temple, the trials believers would face, and even the shifts that would happen in their environment, their next question likely would've been, "When is this going to happen?!" Before they could even ask it, Jesus addressed this question with an illustration.

As mentioned before, there are multiple instances in Scripture when Jesus used fig trees as an illustration. While the fig tree held different symbolism in other passages, here it was likely a simple and accessible example of how to mark the passage of time and the coming season. Jesus told them that when all the signs had taken place, the next age would arrive.

2. **Review 13:30.** Fill in the blank below:

"Truly, I say to you, _____ will not pass away until all these things take place."

Over time, Bible scholars have reached various conclusions about what "this generation" meant: the disciples at the time, the disciples still alive in AD 70 when the temple was destroyed, the Jewish people when the modern-day nation of Israel was formed, the people who will be alive when the tribulation begins, Christians, non-Christians, humanity in general . . . and more. Some of these we already know are wrong, because Christ hasn't come back yet and those who were alive at that time are already dead. As for the others, we don't know yet. So we hold our interpretations with open hands.

The most commonly held view today is that it refers to the church—that Jesus was saying the "generation" of true believers will continue to exist until His return. However, if we insist on the certainty of our interpretations of secondary or tertiary issues, no matter how well-researched or articulated, we miss the main point. So what is the main point? The next verse tells us.

3. **Review 13:31.** Fill in the blank below:

"Heaven and earth will pass away, but _____ will not pass away."

God loves His kids, and He gave us His Word. It will last through the present evil age, and it will last when the age ends. When everything else fails and falls apart—from nature to world leaders—His Word is steadfast. We don't need to cling to our ideas about the timing of the end times. We need to cling to His Word.

Jesus gave His disciples signs to look for, but human nature tells us that they probably still wanted a date and time. Again, before they could even ask, Jesus beat them there.

4. **Review 13:32–37.** Who doesn't know "that day or that hour"? Who does?

It's important to note here that Jesus's statement wasn't a denial of His everlasting divinity, but an affirmation of His temporary humanity. If the disciples needed to know the timing of the end of the age, Jesus would've told them. If we needed to know the timing of the end of the age, God would've told us. But a calendar would impede our faith, not increase it.

It's probably true that every generation of Christians have thought they were living in the end times—and that's a good thing. If we *think* we are living in the end times, then we'll live like we *are*. That doesn't mean our minds should be calculating or our hearts should be anxious. In Mark 13, there are over a dozen imperatives that give us instruction on how to be prepared for the end times. They tell us how to live while we wait for the day of His glorious return.

5. For each verse below, write the instruction Jesus gave.

13:11 _____

13:23 _____

13:35 _____

13:37 _____

As we wrap up this chapter, let's revisit a question you answered yesterday: "What do the words *end times* make you feel? Anxiety, frustration, excitement, curiosity, something else?"

6. Has your answer changed after two days of study?

No matter what our convictions, beliefs, or feelings are about the end times, believers can rejoice. He came. He's coming again. And He's where the joy is!

7. What stood out to you most in this week's study? Why?

8. What did you learn or relearn about God and His character this week?

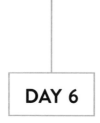

DAY 6

Corresponding Psalm & Prayer

 **READ PSALM 102**

1. What correlation do you see between Psalm 102 and this week's study of Jesus and His kingdom?

2. What portions of this psalm stand out to you most?

3. Close by praying this prayer aloud:

Father,

You are the God who is never too busy to listen to me. You are always engaged in everything happening in my life—You see it all and You understand it better than even I do. Thank You for that! It's

215

such a comfort to know that the things I face today aren't beyond Your care or Your control.

But I confess that it's easy for me to lose heart sometimes. I grow fearful of the end instead of feeling excited about Your Son's return and telling people about His salvation. I strategize to avoid pain and remain in control. I've wallowed in self-pity as though there is no hope. I get bogged down in the never-ending stresses and trials of my life. I've let loneliness and despair crush me instead of looking to You for my purpose and joy. And I repent. Help me to turn from my sins and walk in Your righteous ways instead. Your ways are better, God!

Help me to long for Your Son's return. Give me eyes that see Your blessings, ears that hear Your words of encouragement, and a heart that loves You above all else. Where I've been self-focused, lead me out of that space and give me awareness of those around me who I can serve. Be glorified to conform me to the image of Your Son, Jesus, through the power of Your Spirit, who lives in me.

I surrender my life to You, Lord—every moment of my day, each decision I make, I yield my will and way to Your perfect will and way.

I love You too. Amen.

DAY 7

Rest, Catch Up, or Dig Deeper

 **WEEKLY CHALLENGE**

In Mark 12:28–31, Jesus recited the Shema, originally found in Deuteronomy 6:4–5. He pointed to its message when referencing the two commandments that undergird the Old Testament and display the heart of God. This week, research the Shema using a study Bible, commentary, or other trusted source. Then, create a piece of visual art featuring the Shema. Place it somewhere you'll see it, and practice praying it every day.

— Scripture to Memorize —

And Jesus said to him, "What do you want me to do for you?" And the blind man said to him, "Rabbi, let me recover my sight."

Mark 10:51

Mark 14:
The Heart of the Servant

DAILY BIBLE READING

Day 1: Mark 14:1–11
Day 2: Mark 14:12–25
Day 3: Mark 14:26–42
Day 4: Mark 14:43–65
Day 5: Mark 14:66–72
Day 6: Psalm 26
Day 7: Catch-Up Day

Corresponds to Day 313 of *The Bible Recap.*

WEEKLY CHALLENGE

See page 240 for more information.

Mark 14:1–11

 **READ MARK 14:1–11**

As today's reading opened, important dates on the Jewish calendar were quickly approaching.

1. **Read Exodus 13:3–10 and Leviticus 23:4–8. Using the text and a commentary answer the questions below.**

When did the celebrations take place?

How long did the celebrations last?

What was being commemorated or celebrated?

Where did the events take place, and who was expected to participate?

The population of Jerusalem temporarily swelled as devout Jews made the annual pilgrimage to observe God's appointed feasts. As the religious leaders of the nation, the chief priests and scribes should've been focused on preparing themselves and the people for the events ahead. But instead, they were plotting to kill Jesus secretly.

2. Why might the religious authorities have feared an uproar if they didn't have Jesus arrested and assassinated in secret?

While they were plotting against Jesus, Simon the leper was hosting Him for a dinner party in the nearby village of Bethany—a two-mile walk from Jerusalem.

3. Read Leviticus 13:45–46. What had to have been true about Simon for these festivities to be taking place?

Many scholars believe that Simon had been healed by Jesus at some point. And on a previous trip to Bethany, Jesus had raised Lazarus from the dead (John 12:1–2). So it's a popular belief that this was a party thrown in celebration of Jesus's miraculous power. Simon's house was filled with people who had been served by the goodness of Jesus in unforgettable ways.

4. In what ways have the goodness and power of Jesus transformed your life? Be specific.

The festivities turned awkward when a woman identified as Mary of Bethany (see John 12:3) did something unexpected, dividing the room. Her act is noteworthy in more than a few ways, but we'll look at three.

First, she was a *woman*. In that day, the only culturally appropriate reason for a woman to interrupt dinner was to do something related to serving the meal.

Second, she came with a flask of *pure nard*. Spices, ointments, and oils were often used as investments in Jesus's day because they were portable and easily sold as top-tier imports. The amount she had was valued at roughly three hundred denarii—a year's wages.

Third, she *broke* the alabaster flask. She didn't intend to only use a portion of the expensive perfume on Jesus and save the rest to use later.

5. Review 14:4–9 and fill out the chart below.

Verse	Thought / Response	Action
14:4–5		
14:6–9		

Instead of condemning Mary's actions as a waste, Jesus commended her for her worship. The words translated as "beautiful thing" in the ESV are the Greek words *kalos* and *ergon*, which mean "good work" or "good deed." Jesus wasn't simply saying Mary had done something thoughtful and sweet—He was communicating that what she had done was morally right and pure. In fact, He said the story of her extravagant display of devotion would spread to the ends of the earth alongside the gospel. The fact that you read this story in the Bible today is a fulfillment of Jesus's words!

6. Have you ever been concerned that the way you follow Jesus might be perceived by others as strange or wrong?

It's important to be aware that Jesus wasn't dismissing the value of serving the poor. He didn't fall prey to the "What about . . . ?" argument. He reminded the disciples that the problem of poverty would continue and there would be plenty of opportunities for them to practice God-honoring generosity in every realm.

Some believe Mary truly understood what was about to happen to Jesus, while others say it was just a well-timed expression of love. Either way, Jesus used her act to direct everyone's attention toward His death. After her beautiful expression of sacrifice, one of His very own disciples—Judas Iscariot—decided to assist the religious leaders in the plot to kill Jesus. John's account of this story (John 12:4–6) reveals that Judas was one of those who opposed Mary's actions. In these back-to-back events, two people who had witnessed the power and goodness of Jesus had wildly different responses to Him.

7. How is it possible for two people to witness the same event yet respond to it in opposite ways?

Mark 14:12–25

READ MARK 14:12–25

With the final days of His life in view, Jesus participated in a Passover celebration with His disciples. And though they didn't grasp it, He revealed that what was foreshadowed in the Passover would be fulfilled in His impending death.

1. **Read Mark 11:1–6, then review Mark 14:12–16.** What parallels do you notice?

Jesus sent two disciples to Jerusalem at the most crowded time of the year to look for a needle in a haystack. But they took Jesus at His word, followed His specific instructions, and found everything exactly as He had said, down to the last detail.

2. What do you think the two disciples learned or had reinforced about Jesus through this experience?

The Passover meal was traditionally a time of celebration, but Jesus had news to share: He was going to be betrayed by a man who was at the table with them. One by one, each of the disciples asked if it was them. They each considered the possibility that they might be the one to turn their back on Him. They all were capable of the same kind of sin as Judas.

3. When you think of your own sin, do you tend to think of it as a moral failure or as a betrayal of Jesus?

Although what was about to happen was a fulfillment of prophecy, Jesus still spoke words of woe over Judas. An important principle is at play here. Judas made a willful choice to participate in the plan to put Jesus to death, but Jesus attributed sovereignty over what was going to happen to the eternal purposes of God as revealed in Scripture.

God is never caught by surprise. He's in complete control of everything that happens in the world. He doesn't enact or endorse evil, but He allows it to exist as a necessary consequence of humanity's fall into sin. The reality of God's sovereignty doesn't take away human responsibility and guilt for sinful actions. However, in His great goodness, He's able to take the threads of even the most heinous sins and weave them into His beautiful story of redemption—for our ultimate joy and for His glory (Romans 8:28).

4. What parts of your story do you feel like God's redemption hasn't reached yet?

In 14:22–24, Jesus instituted what we know as the Lord's Supper, Communion, or the Eucharist. In doing this, He gave the disciples a physical practice that could connect them to spiritual realities.

Everything eaten during a Passover meal already had symbolism, so it wouldn't have been shocking when Jesus said that the bread and wine at the dinner had a deeper meaning. But what *was* shocking was what they symbolized—His body and blood—and how they represented the new covenant Jesus was ushering in with this meal.

5. **Read about the old covenant in Deuteronomy 30:15–18, then read about the new covenant in Jeremiah 31:31–34.** How is the new covenant different?

In this new understanding of Passover, the Suffering Servant would be slaughtered, and His blood would be applied to all who believe in His sinless life and sacrificial death as payment for their sin. God would "pass over" those people because He poured out His wrath on Jesus in their place.

When Jesus spoke these words, it was no small thing. No human can bring a new covenant between God and man into existence. In reinterpreting this meal, Jesus emphasized His authority as the Son of God who is equal to the Father.

Though He foretold His death, He also spoke with anticipation about His return. God's plan of salvation and redemption involves His people participating in yet another meal. On "that day" Jesus spoke of, all people who have received cleansing from sin through His blood will be invited to a great banquet. There, the group of believers from across all time and every culture—known as the bride of Christ—will celebrate being united to Him and the privilege of spending eternity in His presence and kingdom (Revelation 19:6–9, 21:1–4).

DAY 3

Mark 14:26–42

 **READ MARK 14:26–42**

Keeping with Passover tradition, the hymn mentioned in 14:26 was likely taken from the Hallel Psalms (Psalms 113–118). *Hallel* means "praise," so it's highly probable that some of the last words on Jesus's lips before He went to Mount Olives were words of praise.

1. **Look at the words of Psalms 116–118.** What common or significant themes do you notice?

The disciples had accepted that Jesus was going to be betrayed by *one* of them, but they had a hard time hearing they would all abandon Him. Jesus wasn't making an educated guess about what would happen—this had been prophesied. The disciples scattering like sheep was a reference to Zechariah 13:7–9. The entire chapter paints a picture of God's people being cleansed from sin in connection with judgment falling on a good shepherd.

    Peter was convinced of the strength of his resolve to follow Jesus, but Jesus, knowing the truth, shared specific details about how things would play out for Peter. In denial of his denial, Peter doubled down, adding that he'd sooner die than desert Jesus. The other disciples followed suit.

As Christ-followers, it can be easy to overestimate our ability to avoid sin and underestimate the difficulty of remaining faithful to Jesus when trials and temptations come.

2. **Read 1 Corinthians 10:12–14.** How can the apostle Paul's words to a group of struggling believers keep you sober minded and give you encouragement in this area?

3. **Look up the word *Gethsemane* (14:32) in a Hebrew lexicon.** What does it mean?

At the base of Mount Olives, there's an olive grove known as the garden of Gethsemane. It sits across the valley that lies just outside the gates of Jerusalem. Jesus took Peter, James, and John with Him as He labored in prayer in this place known as the "olive press." Here, heavy stones were laid on the fruit to extract their valuable oil—which was a fitting foreshadowing of the crushing Jesus would endure to produce something of eternal value.

4. **Review 14:33–36.** Fill out the table below to indicate where you see Jesus's humanity and humility highlighted in these verses.

Humanity	Humility

Jesus's anguish was connected to knowledge of what "the hour" (14:35) and "the cup" (14:36) meant. It would be wrong to think He was simply afraid of dying. Jesus's terror was rightly directed at the magnitude and severity of judgment that sin demanded. He was the Servant Savior who would usher in eternal life only by taking on the punishment for sinners.

Jesus talked to the Father and honestly expressed His desire to avoid the wrath ahead, yet He ultimately yielded to the Father's plan and the purpose He had come to fulfill. His humanity submitted to His divinity.

The men who, moments earlier, said they would die for Jesus, couldn't even keep themselves awake at His command. Directing His attention initially at Peter, Jesus emphasized the importance of watchfulness and prayer as protection against temptation. He pointed out how weak the flesh can be. Then, as He returned to prayer, the disciples returned to sleep.

5. What can you take away from Jesus's model of persistent prayer and His desire for the disciples to share the same priority?

Jesus woke the disciples a final time to let them know He was about to be arrested. From the garden of Gethsemane, it would be easy to see the crowd coming through the city gates and across the valley, carrying their torches to light the way. In the past, when it wasn't yet time for Him to die, Jesus had miraculously evaded people who wanted to arrest Him (John 7:30, 7:44, and 10:39). But this time, He knew His hour had finally come. And with a willing spirit, empowered through His prayers, He was prepared to face it head on.

Mark 14:43–65

READ MARK 14:43–65

With a false show of respect and friendship—a kiss—Judas identified Jesus to the band of armed temple officials. John 18:3 (NASB) says it was the "Roman cohort," which consisted of anywhere from three hundred to six hundred soldiers. They would've never expected the willing surrender of a legitimate criminal, much less that of an innocent man who knew they wanted Him dead.

Jesus didn't resist His arrest, but He pointed out the irony of the secret late-night mission. Though His response was peaceful, one of the disciples opted for a more violent approach—he cut off the ear of the high priest's servant. In Luke's account of this story (Luke 22:49–51), Jesus not only called for a stop to the violence but doubled down and healed the man's ear! If Jesus wanted or needed defending, the Father was more than capable, but the fulfillment of Scripture and the eternal plan of salvation was contingent on His willing submission (Matthew 26:52–54).

1. Describe a time when you tried to solve a problem or change a circumstance in your own fleshly wisdom. What did you learn about the value of seeking God's perspective or help instead?

One interesting note: In 14:51, Mark mentions a scantily clad young man who followed Jesus and ended up fleeing naked. Many of the authors of Scripture show where they appeared in the stories to give credit to their ability to testify. Because of this, some commentators believe this young man was Mark himself. Read up on the theory in a Bible commentary if you're interested.

Jesus was brought before the Jewish supreme court—made up of high-standing Pharisees and Sadducees—to stand trial, but they didn't have the authority to put Him to death. The Jewish legal system was limited under the Romans. Only the Roman governor, Pilate, reserved the right to execute. If the religious leaders wanted Jesus dead, they'd need to have official charges—proof that Jesus had committed a capital offense under Jewish law—to take to the Roman officials.

Desperate to find Jesus guilty, the Sanhedrin were looking for corroborating negative testimonies. Many witnesses were present for this trial, which is somewhat suspicious given it took place between midnight and 6:00 a.m., when people would typically be asleep. This suggests they may have gone so far as to solicit people to be false witnesses against Jesus. Of all the accusations, only one is explicitly stated in the text.

2. **Review 14:57–58.** What was the accusation?

3. **Read John 2:19–21.** How is what Jesus said different from what He was accused of?

4. What did Jesus mean by His statement?

Under the Romans, destruction of a place of worship was punishable by death. If Jesus had been found guilty of that charge, the religious leaders would've been cleared to kill Him. But even in their earnest attempts, they couldn't get the false accusations to line up.

In the face of being wrongly accused, Jesus didn't lash back at His attackers or try to make His own case for innocence. He remained silent, forgoing even the slightest defense—a perfect picture of Isaiah 53:7.

5. When you experience mistreatment or injustice, what is your initial response?

6. Read 1 Peter 2:18–24. How does this passage demonstrate the response of Jesus and challenge cultural norms? How are you personally challenged?

The chief priest turned to Jesus with questions, perhaps hoping He would say something self-incriminating. When asked directly about His identity, Jesus unequivocally declared that He was the Son of God, quoting specific messianic prophecy from Psalm 110:1 in reference to Himself.

7. Brush up on your understanding of blasphemy. Why did the high priest accuse Jesus of blasphemy for His declaration in 14:62?

It was specifically Jesus's claim to be God that led Him to be condemned to die—a truthful confession the religious leaders were unwilling to receive. Today, lots of people are comfortable with many of Jesus's moral teachings, and even the idea of Him being a miracle worker, but they refuse to accept that He is the one true God.

8. Why does it matter that Jesus was and is more than just a man?

If you know people who consider Jesus to be a positive moral figure, good philosopher, or spiritual teacher, but who reject Him as God, you have a great opportunity to get genuinely (not arrogantly) curious in conversation with them. As we've seen in Scripture and likely in our own lives, solid arguments and even miraculous signs and wonders don't change hearts. But gentle, humble, patient conversations can do wonders of their own (Proverbs 25:15)!

9. How can you try to better understand what led them to their conclusions? What questions might be helpful to ask them?

Jesus was mocked and degraded after the guilty verdict was given. This was only the beginning of the humiliation and suffering He would experience in His commitment to carry out the work that would bring salvation to the world.

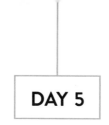

DAY 5

Mark 14:66–72

 READ MARK 14:66–72

We learned in yesterday's reading that Peter, who had initially fled with the other disciples, circled back to keep tabs on Jesus and ended up in the courtyard of the high priest's home, where Jesus was standing trial (Mark 14:50–54). Whether fueled by courage or curiosity, Peter found a spot near the trial and waited to see how things would pan out (Matthew 26:58). When he couldn't blend in like he seemed to have hoped to—his rural accent revealed he was an outsider—a series of confrontations followed.

1. Fill in the chart below with the details of Peter's three denials of Jesus.

	Denial #1	Denial #2	Denial #3
Who is doing the accusing?			
What is the accusation?			
How does Peter respond?			

After being spotted by a servant of the chief priests and asked about his association with Jesus, Peter moved to another spot. Presumably trying to get away at this first sign of trouble, Peter seemed to have missed the first sound of a rooster crowing—the warning that Jesus's words were coming to pass. With each accusation, the stakes got higher as the number of people involved and their certainty that Peter was one of Jesus's disciples grew.

2. Peter's third denial of Jesus in 14:71 included shockingly strong language. What does it mean that "he began to invoke a curse on himself and to swear"?

Cursing doesn't imply that Peter spewed off expletives, attempting to be more convincing. In his cultural context, swearing was functionally pledging an oath, and by invoking a curse he was adding enforceable terms to his false vow of honesty. Peter would have been saying something to the effect of, "I swear I don't know Jesus! May God strike me dead if I'm not telling the truth." When the second rooster crowed, Peter wept as he remembered Jesus's words. He was devastated by the realization of what he'd done.

Jesus had walked closely with Peter for several years. Peter was one of the first disciples called and part of the circle of three men whom Jesus often gave more focused attention and allowed into specific experiences. Peter was often the first to make a bold profession or take a step out in faith, but we also know he messed up in major ways—his flesh was weak and his faith was imperfect. Through it all, Jesus was committed to the process of building him up in understanding of and dependence on Himself as the object and source of his faith. And the occasion of his denial was no different.

3. Have you ever been tempted to believe that you could spiritually "arrive"—rising above trials and temptations? How is that line of thinking harmful to your relationship with God?

When Peter denied Jesus, he was brought back to an acute awareness of just how spiritually poor he was, but his failure didn't have the final word. Jesus had already prepared the way for his restoration and continued purpose and had spoken about it even before he fell away.

Even in our most earnest attempts at faithfulness, we will all fall short; but like Peter, we have access to forgiveness, strength, and purpose in the kingdom when we turn to Jesus again in repentance and faith. God calls us *and* keeps us by His power. He sustains and fulfills everything He initiates—including every aspect of His relationship with us! And it's our greatest blessing in life and in death, because He's where the joy is!

4. What stood out to you most in this week's study? Why?

5. What did you learn or relearn about God and His character this week?

DAY 6

Corresponding
Psalm & Prayer

READ PSALM 26

1. What correlation do you see between Psalm 26 and this week's study of Jesus and His kingdom?

2. What portions of this psalm stand out to you most?

3. Close by praying this prayer aloud:

Father,
You are a God of steadfast love. Your forgiveness drenches my sins in the blood of Your Son, Jesus, and washes them away. Jesus, You demonstrated perfect humility in Your journey to the cross—even

238

singing songs of worship on the way to Your arrest—and I praise You for it.

I confess that I don't walk in that kind of humility. Like the disciples, there have been times when I've arrogantly believed I'm beyond sin. Like Judas, I've valued the wrong things. Like Peter, James, and John, I've chosen to ignore Your warnings at times and been lulled to sleep.

Grant me wisdom, Father. Help me to walk in integrity in the midst of other saints, sinners, and accusers. Give me words of praise in my trials—words that point to You and Your goodness, words that will draw others to You!

I surrender my life to You, Lord—every moment of my day, each decision I make, I yield my will and way to Your perfect will and way.

I love You too. Amen.

Rest, Catch Up, or Dig Deeper

🫙 WEEKLY CHALLENGE

Spiritual victories and failures will be part of all our stories. In the ups and downs of our journeys, it's important that we aren't led to places of self-confidence based on what we do or places of shame based on where we fail. Both destinations take our eyes off Jesus and put them on ourselves, because they are different sides of the same pride coin.

This week, do some research to find a verse that reminds you that any spiritual strength you see in your life comes from God. Remembering the source of our strength and good deeds will serve us well regardless of whether we're more inclined toward arrogance or shame.

Write the verse somewhere you know you'll see it multiple times throughout your day. Let it serve as a reminder of the source of your strength!

Mark 15–16:
The Servant's Sacrifice

Scripture to Memorize

And Jesus said to him, "Go your way; your faith has made you well." And immediately he recovered his sight and followed him on the way.

Mark 10:52

DAILY BIBLE READING

Day 1: Mark 15:1–15

Day 2: Mark 15:16–32

Day 3: Mark 15:33–47

Day 4: Mark 16:1–8

Day 5: Mark 16:9–20

Day 6: Psalm 110

Day 7: Catch-Up Day

Corresponds to Days 316 and 318 of *The Bible Recap*.

WEEKLY CHALLENGE

See page 263 for more information.

Mark 15:1–15

READ MARK 15:1–15

In this week's reading, we'll study the pinnacle of our faith—our Servant Savior's ultimate act of service. Don't rush through this text. Don't be in a hurry to complete questions or to just "get it done." Instead, spend time really letting these events sink in.

Jesus had been tried before the Jewish religious leaders, but they had no authority to enact the death penalty. So they elevated His case to the Roman political leaders. Jesus's next trial was in front of Pilate, the governor Rome had established in the region of Judea. Pilate lived in Caesarea Maritima, but he was temporarily in Jerusalem to keep a watch over the Passover festivities. Because the primary purpose of his role was to maintain order, and the Passover could provide an opportunity for Jews to disrupt Roman order, he made this seventy-five-mile journey to Jerusalem, which would've taken about four days. It was likely not long after his arrival when he was presented with Jesus's case. Pilate asked Jesus if He was the King of the Jews.

1. Why might the Jewish leaders have presented "King of the Jews" as Jesus's charge before Pilate?

While the religious leaders were offended at Jesus's claims to be the Son of God (14:61–62), claiming to be God probably meant nothing to Pilate.

The Romans had lots of gods. Pilate might've thought, *This guy seems fine. What's wrong with one more god?* But claiming to be another king was a political threat to Rome, and Rome had no tolerance for threats.

2. Read Isaiah 53:7. How does Jesus's response in 15:5 show a fulfillment of Old Testament prophecy?

Jesus chose not to respond to any accusations about Him in front of His accusers. He remained silent. When sheep are sheared, they stand in a slightly inclined position—upright on their bottom—and they become so relaxed by the shearing process that they're quiet and almost limp. There isn't drama or excessive noise. Jesus didn't boldly defend Himself like He could have. He knew what was before Him, and He was willing to pay the price. And Pilate was amazed.

Shortly after this, there was a feast where the crowd was presented with one of Pilate's personal traditions: Pardon one prisoner and set him free. This tradition—though it belonged to the Roman governor—was foreshadowed by God's instructions for the Jewish Day of Atonement (also called Yom Kippur).

3. Read Leviticus 16:7–22. Compare it to Mark 15:6–15 and complete the table below. Use your preferred Bible study tool for additional help.

Animal	What It Represents	Person
Goat who was slaughtered (sacrificial goat)		
Goat who was set free (scapegoat)		

4. Using your favorite Bible study tool, look up the meaning of Barabbas's name and circle it below.

    A. son of a shepherd

    B. a man who is a rabbi

    C. son of the father

    D. a prisoner

The two goats symbolized two important things that have to be done with our sin. Our sin must be punished. It can't be ignored. The sacrificial goat represented the innocent dying for the guilty. Jesus will forever be the greatest example of the innocent dying for the guilty.

The second goat, the scapegoat, was driven away into the wilderness. This symbolized something equally important: the guilt and burden of our sin removed from us. Barabbas, full of guilt, was released when he deserved death. We are like Barabbas. We're full of sin and have been declared guilty, but like Barabbas, we too have been set free because our many sins are covered by the blood of Jesus.

Barabbas, son of the father, gained freedom, while *the* Son of *the* Father was sentenced to death. Jesus, though completely blameless, was condemned, while a true criminal—a thief and a murderer—was set free. The religious leaders stirred up the crowd to release the wrong son. Though Pilate found no reason to crucify Jesus, he gave in to the zealous crowd. And afterward, the true Son was scourged.

5. Use a Bible dictionary to define *scourged*.

We probably couldn't stand to witness the atrocity of this type of beating. In fact, we might not even be able to fathom it today. The Romans were professionals at torture and brutality. They studied the most horrific forms of punishment and spared no expense. Jesus, the blameless friend of sinners, was beaten mercilessly.

6. Pause for sixty seconds to think about what Jesus endured on your behalf. Then write a short prayer of gratitude for His great love and His willing submission.

Mark 15:16–32

 **READ MARK 15:16-32**

In yesterday's reading, Pilate wanted to release Jesus. The governor had found no fault in Him, but the crowds chose to release the criminal Barabbas, and Jesus was sentenced to death by crucifixion. Meanwhile, a battalion of Roman soldiers—six hundred men—were called to secure the palace. Rome was determined that no "King of the Jews" would overthrow their government, yet the Messiah, who had the power to silence the seas and the authority to command all demons, willingly remained in custody. They mocked and mistreated Him, and the cruelty of their actions fully displayed that our Suffering Savior was willing to endure in obedience to the Father and for the sake of the lost.

1. **Review Mark 15:17–19.** Match the action of the soldiers with the mocking it communicated.

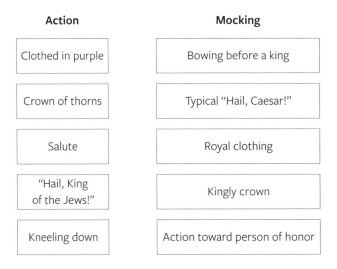

Action	Mocking
Clothed in purple	Bowing before a king
Crown of thorns	Typical "Hail, Caesar!"
Salute	Royal clothing
"Hail, King of the Jews!"	Kingly crown
Kneeling down	Action toward person of honor

Jesus was mocked with the very color purple He helped create, and the thorns that were surely crushed into His scalp were the very thorns He made (John 1:1–3). He wasn't just the King of the Jews—He is the King of kings. He went willingly as they led Him to be crucified.

2. **Read Mark 8:34–38. Read Galatians 2:20.** What does it mean that you are crucified with Christ?

3. How have you chosen to deny yourself, take up your cross, and follow Jesus?

Jesus made His way to the cross knowing that He alone would make a way to the Father through the cross. Often, criminals would be paraded naked down the path to the site of crucifixion, with their hands tied to their wooden crossbar, weighing anywhere from 75–125 pounds. Jesus was too weary to carry the crossbar, so they summoned Simon of Cyrene to assist Him.

4. Why didn't Jesus drink the wine and myrrh offered to Him?

    A. He wasn't thirsty

    B. He knew He was going to die soon and hydration didn't seem important

    C. He chose to face what was before Him with a clear mind

Women of Jerusalem provided a strong, narcotic-like drink to those who were suffering a cruel death to ease their pain. Proverbs 31:6–7 says, "Give strong drink to the one who is perishing, and wine to those in bitter distress; let them drink and forget their poverty and remember their misery no more." Myrrh oil contains compounds that interact with opioid receptors in the brain, which override pain and provide a sedative effect. It seems that Jesus wanted to remain sober minded for all that was before Him.

5. Use a Bible dictionary to define *crucifixion*. You can also read historical sources if they help you gain a deeper understanding of this event.

Crucifixion was brutal. The Romans studied how to make this form of punishment as appalling as possible and spent five hundred years perfecting it. During that time frame, they reportedly performed tens of thousands of crucifixions. In that sense, Jesus's manner of death was not abnormal—He wasn't even the only one killed in that spot on that day—He was hung between two other criminals. His crossbeam was likely nailed on a tree whose trunk had been stripped of its branches, used repeatedly by Rome in their torture factory as a means of more efficient death.

Rome made sure these scenes took place in prominent locations—often on main highways into the city—so that passersby could observe, taunt, and be warned not to disobey Rome. Although surely many people had died on that same tree before Him, and many more would come after Him—some of them perhaps innocent of the crimes they'd been accused of—He was the only truly guiltless man who has ever lived and died. In His final hours, Jesus was mocked, accused, and doubted. Yet His heart remained steadfast. "For the joy set before him he endured the cross" (Hebrews 12:2 NIV).

Mark 15:33–47

 **READ MARK 15:33–47**

While the Servant Savior hung suffering on the cross, the whole land grew dark for three hours—from noon until 3:00 p.m. It's as if creation was groaning alongside its Creator. The lack of light wasn't coincidental, though many throughout history have tried to say that it was. Passover always occurs during a full moon, making a natural eclipse of the sun impossible.

This weather phenomenon isn't recorded only in Scripture. As historian Julius Africanus tells us, the Roman historian Phlegon recorded these events but wrongly attributed the cause: "Phlegon records that, in the time of Tiberius Caesar, at full moon, there was a full eclipse of the sun from the sixth hour to the ninth."[*]

1. **Use a Bible study tool to find what times the sixth hour and ninth hour occurred.**

---

[*]Julius Africanus, "Fragment xviii," The Writings of Julius Africanus, Bible Hub, https://biblehub.com/library/africanus/the_writings_of_julius_africanus/fragment_xviii_on_the_circumstances.htm#1.

At 3:00 p.m., Jesus cried out, "Eloi, Eloi, lema sabachthani?" Some people in the crowd misunderstood what He was saying and used it as fuel for their continual mocking. The soldiers were ruthless; there was no reverence for death and dying when a perceived criminal was on the cross. Clearly, a spiritual darkness existed alongside the actual darkness. How tragic that while prophecy was being fulfilled and humanity was about to be redeemed, many still lacked the eyes to see.

2. **Read Psalm 22. Using a Bible commentary or other Bible study tool, describe the significance of Jesus's words in 15:34.**

Psalms are meant to be sung. The Bible had not yet been divided into chapters, so yelling out "Psalm 22!" would not have made the crowds unroll their scrolls to that passage. Instead, Jesus cried out the first line, pointing people to this well-known messianic psalm. While on the cross, He served the brutal crowds and remained obedient to the Father by pointing to the good news before His final breath.

3. Complete the chart below to display statements showing how Mark's gospel reveals the fulfillment of Psalm 22 in Jesus's life and ministry.

Psalm 22 Passage	Mark 15 Passage	Fulfillment in Christ
Verse 1	Verse 34	
Verse 7		Jesus is scorned and despised
Verse 16	Verse 27	
Verse 18	Verse 24	

After Jesus cried out, someone—a bystander or a Roman soldier—offered Jesus a drink of sour wine. It's not entirely clear in Scripture whether that person's motive was continued mockery and mistreatment or mercy, but the circumstances seem to indicate it was the former. It's important to note that the "sour wine drink" is different from the narcotic-like drink Jesus refused earlier (15:23). This drink was more like wine vinegar, a common beverage used by soldiers and laborers because it relieved thirst more effectively than water and it was relatively inexpensive. John's gospel describes Jesus taking a drink before He uttered a phrase and stopped breathing (John 19:30).

4. Review 15:38. What took place as Jesus took His last breath? What is the significance of this major change in the temple? Read Hebrews 10:19–20 for additional insight.

The veil in the temple was torn from top to bottom! No man could have done this. Imagine the shock of the priest who first saw it. This curtain—reportedly three inches thick and made of animal skins—hung between the Holy Place and the Holy of Holies, where the presence of God dwelled. This curtain marked off a spot that was so set apart the high priest was only allowed to enter it once a year. But as Jesus's death fulfilled the Father's wrath and the new covenant was established, the old ways were no longer needed. Jesus had bridged the gap between a holy God and sinful man, and the barrier was removed!

5. Read Hebrews 4:14–5:10. List three of the things Jesus did in this passage that are most meaningful to you right now.

6. **Read Isaiah 53:9.** What prophetic fulfillment occurred as Joseph of Arimathea took Jesus's body to be buried?

Jesus was buried in a borrowed tomb—a rich man's grave—but He wouldn't stay there. The women watched from a distance, Pilate stood surprised by the timeline of death, and the centurion said, "This man was the Son of God!" In various ways, this event was significant for all those in attendance. Thousands of years later, this moment in time stands as the hinge point of history, and it continues to be significant as humanity dwells on it with awe and wonder.

7. Recall the moment you believed Jesus is who He says He is. Write a brief testimony below.

Mark 16:1–8

 **READ MARK 16:1–8**

Yesterday, we read that Jesus was buried. And today we read that He is no longer in the tomb! Those who followed Jesus were grieved at His death, but those who knew Him well and loved Him surely ached not only over losing Him, but also because He apparently wasn't the Messiah they thought He was.

Mary Magdalene, Mary the mother of James, and Salome waited until after Sabbath ended at sunset to buy spices to anoint Him. On their way, they continued to develop their plan, trying to solve problems in advance— "How will we get inside the tomb?" But as soon as they arrived, they saw that the stone had been rolled away from the entrance.

1. **Read Matthew 27:65–28:2.** What does this passage tell us about how the stone was rolled away?

Matthew's account made it plain that a guard was placed outside the tomb. This tells us that Jesus's disciples did not move the stone away. Even if they were brave enough or strong enough, they likely wouldn't have been able to overcome the armed Roman guards. It seems God used a combination of natural and supernatural elements—an earthquake and an angel—to roll the stone away.

2. **Review 16:5 and read Matthew 28:3–5.** Who was the "young man"? What was the women's response upon seeing him? What was his response to them?

The "young man" is an angel. Every time angels appear in Scripture, they appear as human males. Scripture often describes them as being dressed in white, and their appearance is usually described as "radiant" and "like lightning." There are some Scripture-based theories that angels might be very large, and when they encounter humans they often say, "Fear not." Angels are probably terrifying. And Scripture never describes angels as having wings or halos (though other types of heavenly creatures, cherubim and seraphim, *do* have wings). The women at the tomb were afraid, but he told them not to be alarmed—in fact, they had reason to rejoice, because their Messiah had been resurrected!

3. **Use a dictionary to define** *resurrection* **and** *resuscitation,* **and note the distinct difference between the two.**

4. In the passages below, identify whether the newly alive person was resuscitated or resurrected.

1 Kings 17:22 _____

2 Kings 4:32–35 _____

John 11:41–44 _____

Luke 8:52–55 _____

Luke 7:14–15 _____

Acts 9:40–41 _____

Acts 20:9–10 _____

Each of the people mentioned above was miraculously resuscitated. They were brought back to life in the same body and would eventually die again in the same body. Resurrection isn't just living again—it's living in a new form of our bodies, one that is perfectly suited for eternal life (1 Corinthians 15:35–49). Up to this point, Jesus is the first and only one who has been resurrected into this new life. He's fully alive, right now, in His same body, and He's seated at the right hand of the Father, still doing ministry as He intercedes on our behalf (Hebrews 7:25).

5. **Read 1 Thessalonians 4:14–18, Philippians 3:20–21, and 1 Corinthians 15:49–57.** What promise do these verses contain for those who are in Christ?

Because the promised resurrection of Jesus was fulfilled as Scripture said it would be, we can continue to hope in the promise of our own resurrection. Christ not only died for our sins, but He resurrected so that one day we too may be resurrected!

6. **Review 16:7.** Notice the young man said, "His disciples and Peter." Why do you think he might have made this distinction? **Read Luke 22:61–62 for help with your answer.**

7. Have you ever felt like your bad decisions or sinful behavior disqualified you from being a disciple of Jesus? What hope do you find in knowing that Peter is included too?

The angel gave specific instructions and reminded them that they'd see Jesus just as He'd told them. The women ran away from the tomb, completely overwhelmed and awestruck, and kept silent about what they'd seen.

Mark 16:9–20

 READ MARK 16:9-20

If you're reading in the ESV, you may notice brackets around today's passage. Your Bible might also have a note that this part of the text wasn't included in some earlier manuscripts. Because they do appear in *some* early manuscripts and there is continued debate about whether these verses should be included in Scripture, it's wise to hold them with an open hand. We won't scream where Scripture whispers. At the same time, we can rest assured knowing that most of the information in these passages is also included throughout the other three gospel accounts.

It's worth noting that Jesus's first appearance to a human after His resurrection was to a woman who was formerly demonized. This was a big deal in first-century Israel. Her testimony would not have been considered reliable because she was a woman, yet Jesus entrusted her with the greatest news of all. For a moment, she was the only person in what would eventually be called the church. This woman who had formerly been demonized by seven demons—until Jesus transformed her—carried the message of *His* transformation to the others.

1. How did the disciples respond when Mary told them she'd seen Jesus alive?

After appearing to Mary Magdalene, Jesus appeared to two other men, who went back and told the disciples.

2. How did the disciples respond when the two travelers shared about their encounter with Jesus?

3. **Using a Greek lexicon, look up the word *rebuked* from 16:14.** What does this tell you about Jesus's attitude toward His disciples?

This word *rebuked* here is more like a stern admonishment. He was correcting them because of their unbelief and hardness of heart. He had told them repeatedly that He would be raised from the dead, yet when multiple messengers shared the news, they didn't believe. It appears their doubt wasn't in the messengers, but in the Lord. Jesus, who would be leaving soon, knew they had a weighty calling that would require their faith to be fully formed.

4. Are there any areas where your heart is lacking a full commitment to the mission of Jesus? Identify these places below and write a prayer of repentance, asking God to change your heart.

The final section of Mark's gospel is known as the Great Commission. Some scholars believe this commission was only for Jesus's eleven disciples, but the prominent belief within orthodox Christianity is that it applies to all followers of Jesus for all time.

Jesus shared very specific information with them, but the only command they were given was "Go into all the world and proclaim the gospel to the whole creation." This instruction was certainly countercultural for a people who were accustomed to being God's chosen people, who practiced isolating themselves from outsiders. But Jesus had spent His three years of ministry demonstrating God's love for people outside their own regions and nationalities. He had lived out what the Old Testament prophets foretold: God wants to rescue people from among every nation (Isaiah 19:19–25, 56:7)! Jesus called the disciples to leave their inner circles and share the good news with people outside of their culture and comfort zone.

5. How does this command shape your life as a disciple of Jesus? Share an example of how you live this out, or share what you'd like to do differently to better live out His calling.

The one portion of this text that doesn't appear in any other gospels is in 16:17–18. It's worth noting that—even in this passage—the believers aren't commanded to do these things; Jesus said those things would happen as a result of believing and obeying. And He assured them that they'd be protected as they stepped into dangerous territory.

6. Review 16:19–20. Referencing a Bible study tool, describe in your own words what it means that Jesus is seated at the right hand of the Father.

You can rest assured knowing that Jesus is seated at the right hand of God. He has finished His saving work! And while we await His return, we imitate His servanthood. We can serve our neighbors and the nations as we serve our Savior. He was more than just an example of how to serve; He is the very one who makes all good service possible (Philippians 1:6, 2:13). He does the doing—in and through us. And He's where the joy is!

7. What stood out to you most in this week's study? Why?

8. What did you learn or relearn about God and His character this week?

Corresponding Psalm & Prayer

 READ PSALM 110

1. What correlation do you see between Psalm 110 and this week's study of Jesus and His kingdom?

2. What portions of this psalm stand out to you most?

3. Close by praying this prayer aloud:

Father,

    From before creation, You have always been God—Father, Son, and Spirit. You have always existed in perfect love. Before You even invented time, You already had a redemption plan for Your people, and I praise You for including me in that—for redeeming me and adopting me into Your family!

I confess that it's easy for me to lose sight of what Your Son, Jesus, made available to me: access to a relationship with You, the forgiveness of my sin, a righteous new identity free of shame, the power of Your Spirit living in me, and an inheritance in Your kingdom! I confess that I'm guilty of fixing my eyes on myself—I haven't always felt the desire to share Your good news with those around me. I've grown complacent at times. And I repent.

Change my heart, God. Help me want to share the good news of Jesus. Open up opportunities for me to talk about You with the people in my life, or even strangers I encounter throughout my day. Prompt me with regular reminders of Your goodness. Give me joy where I lack it. Turn my selfishness into servanthood—for Your glory and my joy!

I surrender my life to You, Lord—every moment of my day, each decision I make, I yield my will and way to Your perfect will and way.

I love You too. Amen.

Rest, Catch Up, or Dig Deeper

 **WEEKLY CHALLENGE**

Throughout the study, we've witnessed Jesus continually serve those around Him. Do you seek to imitate Christ through serving like He did? Is your service motivated by gratitude or guilt? How does serving feel different when it's coming from gratitude instead of obligation?

   If you don't have a place to serve, reach out to your local church and ask where the needs are. Prayerfully commit to a regular practice of serving.

Reflect on the following questions as you serve: How did Jesus serve? How does service shape your heart?

FOR GROUP LEADERS

Thank you for using this study and leading others through it as well! Each week has a wide variety of content (content and questions, daily Bible reading, Scripture memorization, weekly challenge, and resources) to help the reader develop a range of spiritual disciplines. Feel free to include as much or as little of that in your meetings as you'd like. The details provided in How to Use This Study (pp. 11–12) will be helpful to you and all your group members, so be sure to review that information together!

It's up to you and your group how you'd like to structure your meetings, but we suggest including time for discussion of the week's study and Bible text, mutual encouragement, and prayer. You may also want to practice your Scripture memory verses together as a group or in pairs. As you share with each other, "consider how to stir up one another to love and good works" (Hebrews 10:24) and "encourage one another and build one another up" (1 Thessalonians 5:11).

Here are some sample questions to help facilitate discussion. This is structured as a weekly study, but if your group meets at a different frequency, you may wish to adjust the questions accordingly. Cover as many questions as time allows, or feel free to come up with your own. And don't forget to check out the additional resources we've linked for you at MyDGroup.org/Resources/Mark.

Sample Discussion Questions

What questions did this week's study or Bible text bring up for you?

What stood out to you in this week's study?

What did you notice about God and His character?

How were you challenged by your study of the Bible text? Is there anything you want to change in light of what you learned?

How does what you learned about God affect the way you live in community?

What correlation did you see between the psalm from Day 6 and this week's study of Jesus and His kingdom?

Have you felt God working in you through the weekly challenge? If so, how?

Is your love for God's Word increasing as we go through this study? If so, how?

Did anything you learned increase your joy in knowing Jesus?

ACKNOWLEDGMENTS

It was my great joy to work alongside a gifted, passionate team of writers on this project. Laura Buchelt, Emily Pickell, Evaline Asmah, Meg Mitchell, and Brittney Rice—thank you for your incredible research, creativity, wisdom, humility, and laughter.

Olivia Le is an invaluable friend and team member who organized this whole process. And Lisa Jackson, my literary agent, provided formative guidance, feedback, and support.

My editors, Jeff Braun and Hannah Ahlfield, are truly the dream team for me. Thank you for sharing this vision to help people unearth more layers of the beauty of God's Word.

And to the rest of the incredible D-Group Team—Rachel Mantooth, Lindsay Ruhter, Warwick Fuller, Omar Cardenas, and Jane Long—our board, and all our leaders and members around the world. I love being on mission with you!

ABOUT THE EDITOR

TARA-LEIGH COBBLE'S zeal for biblical literacy led her to create a network of Bible studies called D-Group (Discipleship Group). Every week, hundreds of men's and women's D-Groups meet in homes, in churches, and online for Bible study and accountability.

She also writes and hosts a daily podcast called *The Bible Recap* designed to help listeners read and understand the Bible in a year. The podcast garnered over three hundred million downloads in its first five years, and more than twenty thousand churches around the world have joined their reading plan to know and love God better. It has been turned into a book published by Bethany House Publishers.

Tara-Leigh is a *Wall Street Journal* bestselling author, speaks to a wide variety of audiences, and regularly leads teaching trips to Israel because she loves to watch others be awed by the story of Scripture through firsthand experience.

Her favorite things include sparkling water and days that are 72 degrees with 55 percent humidity, and she thinks every meal tastes better when eaten outside. She lives in a concrete box in the skies of Dallas, Texas, where she has no pets, children, or anything that might die if she forgets to feed it.

For more information about Tara-Leigh and her ministries, you can visit her online.

Websites: taraleighcobble.com | thebiblerecap.com | mydgroup.org | israelux.com
Social media: @taraleighcobble | @thebiblerecap | @mydgroup | @israeluxtours